W9-BIO-259

AROUND lOndon WITH KIDS

by Jacqueline Brown

Fodor's Travel Publications
New York • Toronto • London • Sydney • Auckland

www.fodors.com

CREDITS
Writer: Jacqueline Brown

Series Editor: Karen Cure
Editor: Andrea Lehman
Editorial Production: Stacey Kulig
Production/Manufacturing: Robert Shields

Design: Fabrizio La Rocca, *creative director*;
Tigist Getachew, *art director*
Illustration and Series Design: Rico Lins, Keren Ora
Admoni/Rico Lins Studio

ABOUT THE WRITER
Between bringing up her two children in London, Jacqueline Brown has worked on a wide range of consumer magazines, including *Yellow Pages City Guides,* and is a frequent contributor to *Fodor's London* and other Fodor's books.

Fodor's Around London with Kids

Copyright © 2001 by Fodors LLC

Fodor's is a registered trademark of Random House, Inc. All rights reserved under International and Pan-American Copyright Conventions. Published in the United States by Fodor's Travel Publications, Inc., a unit of Fodors LLC, a subsidiary of Random House, Inc., New York, and simultaneously in Canada by Random House of Canada Limited, Toronto. Distributed by Random House, Inc., New York.

ISBN 0-679—00726-1
ISSN 1533-5321
First Edition

Important Tip
Although all prices, opening times, and other details in this book are based on information supplied to us at press time, changes occur all the time in the travel world, and Fodor's cannot accept responsibility for facts that become outdated or for inadvertent errors or omissions. So always confirm information when it matters, especially if you're making a detour to visit a specific place.

Special Sales
Fodor's Travel Publications are available at special discounts for bulk purchases for sales promotions or premiums. Special editions, including personalized covers, excerpts of existing guides, and corporate imprints, can be created in large quantities for special needs. For more information, contact your local bookseller or Special Markets, Fodor's Travel Publications, 280 Park Avenue, New York, NY 10017. Inquiries from Canada should be directed to your local Canadian bookseller or sent to Random House of Canada, Ltd., Marketing Dept., 2775 Matheson Boulevard East, Mississauga, Ontario L4W 4P7. Inquiries from the United Kingdom should be sent to Fodor's Travel Publications, 20 Vauxhall Bridge Road, London, England SW1V 2SA.

PRINTED IN THE UNITED STATES OF AMERICA
10 9 8 7 6 5 4 3 2 1

COUNTDOWN TO GOOD TIMES

GET READY, GET SET!

Everyone knows that organizing a family's schedule is a full-time job, whether you're juggling activities at home or planning the perfect vacation. Spending time together shouldn't be another chore to figure out, especially when you're supposed to be relaxing and enjoying yourselves.

We know what it's like to try to find good places to take your children or grandchildren, especially when you're in a strange city with a limited amount of time and energy. Sometimes it's tough to find out when places are open, whether they're likely to be crowded or even sold out, and what age group they're geared to. There's nothing like bringing a "grown-up" 12-year-old to an activity that's intended for his 6-year-old sister. And if you're planning a trip to London, it's harder still to figure out the best things to do before you even get there. That's where we come in.

What you'll find in this book are 68 ways to have a terrific couple of hours or an entire day with children in tow. London is crammed with things for kids to do, particularly now that most of the tried-and-true museums have had a technological facelift. We've scoured the city, digging out activities your kids—and you—will love, from the historic splendor of Hampton Court and Windsor Castle to the hands-on, whiz-bang activities of the Science Museum. The best part is that it's stress-free, uncomplicated, and easy for you. Open the book to any page and find a helpful description of a kid-friendly attraction, with age ratings to make sure it's right for your family, smart tips on visiting so that you can get the most out of your time there, and family-friendly eats nearby. The address, telephone number, open hours, and admission prices are all there, too.

Those with special interests, or anyone who loves tours, should go to the London Tourist Information Centre at Victoria Station Forecourt, or the Britain Visitor Centre (1 Regent St.), near Piccadilly Circus, and scour the shelves for leaflets from independent operators.

WAYS TO SAVE MONEY

We list only regular adult, student (with ID), and kids' prices, in pounds sterling; children under the ages specified are free. In spring 2001, the exchange rate was $1.42 to the pound sterling. It always pays to ask at the ticket booth whether any discounts are offered for a particular status or affiliation (but don't forget to bring your ID). Discounts are often available for senior citizens. Many attractions offer family tickets or long-term memberships. Prices vary, but the memberships often pay for themselves if you visit several times (you can usually convert your first days admission if you do it before you leave). Sometimes there are other perks: newsletters or magazines, members-only previews, and shop discounts.

Look for coupons—which might save you £1 per person or provide a child's free admission—in such magazines as *Kids Out* and the *Evening Standard* summer supplement for kids. Hotel desks often carry Theatre Pair coupons, which allow you to buy two tickets at half price for selected theaters. In addition, some groups of attractions offer combination passes, which are cheaper than paying for separate admissions. One such bargain is the Greenwich Passport, covering the National Maritime Museum, Royal

Observatory, and *Cutty Sark* museum ship. Some London passes cover not only attractions but transportation as well. The London Pass includes around 50 attractions, including Buckingham Palace, Windsor Castle, and boat and bus trips, along with free travel and restaurant discounts. It comes in one-to six-day denominations and starts at £39 adults, £24 children 5–14. You can buy the London Pass on the Web (www.londonpass.com), by phone (tel. 0870/242–9988) before you arrive, or from Tourist Information Centres (at Heathrow Airport and Victoria and Liverpool Street stations) and at London Transport Travel Information Centres.

Also keep an eye out for attractions—mostly museums and galleries—that offer free admission one day a week or after a certain time in the afternoon (usually an hour or two before closing). We've noted several in this book.

WHEN TO GO
With the exception of seasonal attractions, kid-oriented destinations are generally busiest when children are out of school—especially weekends, holidays, and summer—but not necessarily. Attractions that draw school trips can be swamped with clusters of some-times-inconsiderate children tall enough to block the view of your preschooler. But school groups tend to leave by early afternoon, so weekdays after 2 during the school year can be an excellent time to visit museums, zoos, and aquariums. For outdoor attractions, it's good to visit after a rain, since crowds will likely have cleared out.

The hours we list are the basic hours, not necessarily those applicable on holidays. Some attractions are closed when schools are closed, but others add extra hours on these days. It's always best to check if you want to see an attraction on a holiday.

SAFETY

Obviously the amount of vigilance necessary will depend on the attraction and the ages of your kids. In crowded attractions, keep an eye on your children at all times, as their ages warrant. When you arrive, point out to your kids what the staff or security people are wearing, and find a very visible landmark to use as a meeting place, should you get separated. If you do split into groups, pick a time to meet. This will decrease waiting time, help you and your kids get the most out of your time there, and manage everyone's expectations.

LEARNING ENGLISH

So you thought you were fluent in English until you go to your first London restaurant and try to read the menu. Relax. You'll get into the British swing of things in no time. Popular kid's food choices include bangers and mash (sausage and mashed potatoes), fish-and-chips (fried fish and french fries), and, to be extra confusing, crisps (potato chips).

"Brilliant" is an oft-heard word for "wonderful," and "trainers" are "sneakers." As far as transportation goes, "single" means "one-way," and "return" means "round-trip." Make a detective game of it with your kids, and have fun figuring out the meanings of all the phrases you hear. Brilliant.

FINAL THOUGHTS

Actually, this time it's yours, not ours. We'd love to hear what you or your kids thought about the attractions you visited. Or if you happened upon a place that you think warrants inclusion, by all means, send it along, so the next family can enjoy London even more. You can e-mail us at editors@fodors.com (specify the name of the book on the subject line), or write to us at Fodor's Around London with Kids, 280 Park Avenue, 10th floor, New York, NY 10017. We'll put your ideas to good use. In the meantime, have fun!

THE EDITORS

AQUATIC EXPERIENCE

I n the wild west of London's huge Syon Park (*see below*), Aquatic Experience is home to a weird, wonderful collection of exotic and fascinating beasts: saline and freshwater creatures plus a handful of landlubbers. The unifying theme here is that the animals were rescued or represent endangered species, from the thumbnail-size sea horse to lumbering crocodiles. If possible—but obviously not with the aforementioned creatures—you can meet and pet them.

Dedicated keepers, who you get the feeling would probably eat and sleep with their charges if they could, answer questions and encourage you to encounter these well-cared-for animals, each of which has its own personality. Mango the cheerful cockatoo—his gorgeous plumage explains his name—likes to walk on your arm, if you don't mind the occasional pricks from his long claws. If you are very privileged, he might let you caress him under his wing. The monitor lizard, another character, often is taken for a walk in the yard, although he's a little less receptive to petting. The tortoises, however, which lumber about in an open

KEEP IN MIND The nearby London Butterfly House (*see below*) has more than 1,000 butterflies as well as other creepy crawlies. Separate admission is charged. You also have to pay extra to enter Syon's gardens, across the parking lot (*see* Syon Park), but the fabulous space, lakes, and floral and arboreal beauty make it well worth it. If you want to cram in everything, allow a good hour for the Aquatic Experience, another hour for the butterflies, and at last twice that for the park. If you don't have that much time, perhaps some of your group wants to see the butterflies while the rest visits here.

 Syon Park, London Rd., Brentford.
Rail: Syon La.

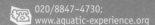 020/8847-4730;
www.aquatic-experience.org

 £3.50 ages 16 and up,
£2.75 children 4-15

 Apr–Sept, daily 10–6; Oct–Mar,
daily 10–5

3 and up

pen, just love attention. At children's parties (animal-encounter parties are favorites here) and other times (check at the admission desk), Ozzie the owl performs flying feats. In one trick, he walks over a line of children lying side by side on the ground—this sometimes proves too much for tiny tots.

The more deadly creatures are kept behind glass, from the tiny, finger-size Amazon frog, which looks cute but emits a deadly poison, to coiled-up pythons and crocs. On the aquatic front, there's a deep tank with koi and catfish where you can feed the fish with the keeper (check at the admission desk for times). In a shallow rock pool, tiny terrapins climb out to greet you, and in the tropical tank, the entrancing sea horses bob up and down.

For some action after all this gazing and encountering, visit the small play area within the Aquatic Experience or head to the wide-open spaces of the park.

EATS FOR KIDS
It's too far to walk to leave Syon Park for lunch, but luckily there are good options within the park (see London Butterfly House).

HEY, KIDS! What's the difference between a crocodile and an alligator? They both belong to the same family group, crocodilians, which have been around since prehistoric times. The way to tell them apart is by their teeth, although since they have eaten humans, you won't want to get close enough to inspect them. But just so you know, alligators don't have those two fiendish lower incisors visible when their jaw is closed. There are also two other related species: caimans, belonging to the alligator group, and the lesser-known gavial, which has a long, slender snout-shape mouth, with plenty of sharp upper teeth visible, even when shut.

ART 4 FUN

Let your imagination go bananas—or dotty, stripey, fishy, or any other way inspiration takes you! At this creative café–cum–art workshop, you can paint onto a mug, plate, eggcup, vase, or any of about 100 other ceramic pieces and make your own souvenir or gift. Expertise is not required, only enthusiasm.

The whole spectrum of colors is available, and friendly assistants are on hand to help you with the basics, such as how to plan your work, the best way to draw outlines, and how to apply dark colors last. You can use brushes, sponges, stencils, or fingertips. For inspiration, browse the examples on walls and shelves, and pay attention to the helpful do's and don'ts. The ceramics (which include some Gucci designs, just to add a touch of exclusivity to your handiwork) are plain biscuit ware, which is then glazed and fired after you're finished designing. The main drawback is that this takes a couple of days, so if you won't be around, you'll have to have the finished work mailed to your home. All ceramic tableware is microwave- and dishwasher-safe.

HEY, KIDS!

The helpful staff at Art 4 Fun won't throw you out if you are too busy having fun. Late-night parties have been known to get pretty colorful. Some children even come in pjs, making a pajama party with a difference.

KEEP IN MIND
The cost of your project is based on the particular piece you choose in addition to a flat studio space fee. This is the most central branch of Art 4 Fun. Others are at 44 Chiswick High Road, W4; 172 West End Lane, West Hampstead, NW6; and 212 Fortis Green Road, Muswell Hill, N10. Details on all of these can be obtained by calling tel. 020/8994–4800.

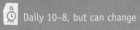

If you want to take a completed piece away with you, how about a super silk tie or a pillowcase? Several designs are available, from bold abstract shapes to a more conservative small repeating pattern. All you have to do is choose the colors and paint them on. You can also make a mosaic picture frame or mirror frame, which involve making color selections and lots of sticking.

The mood at Art 4 Fun is very relaxing. Music plays in the background, and there's the gentle buzz of other people working. If you're hungry, you can buy drinks and snacks to help the creative juices flow. Mom and dad can drink coffee while the kids do all the work, or, more likely, parents can catch the creative bug themselves and grab a paintbrush. You can make an inexpensive family evening out by bringing takeout (if you bring wine, there's a small charge for the corkage) while designing your own dishes.

EATS FOR KIDS While you're in this bohemian area of London, check out the Portuguese quarter. The **Lisboa Pattisserie** (57 Golborne Rd., W10, tel. 020/8968-5242) and **Oporto** (62A Golborne Rd., W10, tel. 020/8968-8839) are typical Portuguese cafés selling budget meals and snacks with lots of atmosphere. For a range of pizzas flat and folded, try **Calzone** (2A Kensington Park Rd., tel. 020/7243-2003).

BANK OF ENGLAND MUSEUM

Step up from the bowels of Bank station into London's traditional commercial heart. You'll be surrounded by the columned edifices that are the Royal Exchange; the Mansion House, the official residence of the Lord Mayor; and the Bank of England. Next, step around the corner to the bank's museum, where you can learn about the history of both the bank and money. Pass through the heavy metal door, and take in the lofty walls and domed ceiling. A gatekeeper in a dapper plum top hat and tails shows you to the museum, but, sadly, he is not your guide. Instead, follow the arrows on the helpful leaflet, and the story of the bank will unfold.

The original interior of the Bank Stock Office, designed by Sir John Soane, has been re-created, complete with heavy wooden cupboard desks, glowing embers in the fireplace, and lifelike clerks and customers from 1734, when Threadneedle Street became the bank's official premises. In many newspaper cartoons, the bank was caricatured as "the old lady of Threadneedle Street"—forever in charge, maintaining discipline when willful kings and governments wanted to spend a lot of money.

EATS FOR KIDS The **Place Below** (Cheapside, tel. 020/7329–0789) is in the vaults of St. Mary-le-Bow church. The atmospheric veggie café serves quiches, pasta dishes, and salad at budget prices. Near the foundations of the Roman Temple of Mithras, **Starbucks** (Unit 10A, No.1 Poultry, tel. 020/7489–1994) sells good coffee and hot chocolate for the tots, well-filled sandwiches, gooey cakes, and muffins. A few steps farther on is **Silks & Spice** (Temple Court, 11 Queen Victoria St., tel. 020/7248–7878), serving pan-Asian food with a practical, budget Oriental Express lunch: one-plate dishes (seafood, meat, or vegetables) with rice for £5–£6.

 Bartholomew La., EC2.
Tube: Bank

 Free

 020/7601–5545 recording;
www.bankofengland.co.uk

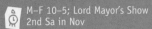 M–F 10–5; Lord Mayor's Show
2nd Sa in Nov

 9 and up

Pick up one of the free activity sheets, designed for different age groups. Kids might be directed to seek out old coins or read stories about famous bank founders, forgers, gold bar prices, or banknote designs. Upon completing the sheet, children get a fun little souvenir.

Throughout the museum, but especially in an area near the end of the tour, videos and touch screens tell the history of the bank and describe its workings today. You can learn how forgers have been outfoxed for centuries by increasingly sophisticated monetary design and about the complications of setting interest rates. A fast-paced game lets you pit your wits in the financial markets. Reckon you could make a killing? You'll have to react to all sorts of obstacles, such as market crashes and natural disasters, to succeed.

KEEP IN MIND
Special activities for kids are organized during summer vacations. You might catch Grunal the money maker in period costume, minting silver pennies while telling golden tales.

HEY, KIDS! Gold was once the foundation of banks, but it was also used to make people feel good—literally! Centuries ago, alchemists mixed powdered gold into drinks to treat arthritis, and it is still used to ease the complaint today. If you want to feast your eyes on gold bars, there are a couple of stacks here. Compare different types by price and weight. Browsing through the coin cases, you might be surprised by how big and thick some coins were. It would feel pretty good to have a handful of those coins jangling in your pocket, now wouldn't it?

BBC EXPERIENCE

I f you or your children have ever longed to commentate on a soccer match, work a television camera, or edit a soap opera, here's your lucky break. What's more, you get to display your talent at the world-famous BBC and learn a bit about its storied history.

The British Broadcasting Corporation has been around for more than 75 years. It was the first nationwide voice for radio and, later, for television. (Remember that before TV was affordable for most Brits, the "wireless" provided both entertainment and news from their backyard and beyond.) The BBC has been *the* information source in times of trouble and triumph, including World War II, the queen's coronation, and the moon landings. A guided tour—separate from the many interactive areas you'll want to explore unaided—touches on these landmark events.

Before you reach the hands-on area, get an in-depth look at how a recent hit drama or series is put together. Then, have fun. Be an operator on a radio program. There are

KEEP IN MIND Remind your kids that the archive clips of comedy, drama, and music are quintessentially British. So they might find some things hard to understand and the humor a little quirky.

HEY, KIDS! Today's top daytime radio music shows may sound smooth and seamless, but there's a team of people frenetically working in the studio to achieve that impression. The main deejay may be backed up by another deejay lining up the tracks, with a producer and other technical staffers helping, too. When it works well, it all sounds cool and easy. If you took part in the radio drama simulation, you'll know how nerve-racking it can be to put on a show when you're following a script. Imagine how hard it must be to do it off-the-cuff, the way most deejays do.

 Broadcasting House, Portland Pl., W1.
Tube: Oxford Circus

 020/7765-1109;
www.bbc.co.uk/experience

 £7.50 ages 16 and up,
£5.95 students,
£6.50 children 5–15

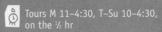 Tours M 11–4:30, T–Su 10–4:30,
on the ½ hr

 8 and up

lots of buttons to press as you try to follow a drama's script and the director's cues. You'll discover how sound effects, such as opening doors and gunshots, are made today. In the good old days, the real thing was used; now it's all computerized.

You can try your hand in a puppet TV show or work behind the scenes, operating a television camera and panning and zooming in on London sights. Using music software, you can produce your own pop classic on CD, or check out the latest rock and pop news on the Radio One Web site.

If you think you're ready for the big time, try hosting the weather forecast. It's not as easy as it looks. You have to point at a map of the British Isles (behind you) while facing the camera. Don't worry if your geography is a little rusty; even natives point into the sea when they mean to point toward London. Then watch a bloopers tape in which even super-cool professionals blunder. Everyone makes mistakes.

EATS FOR KIDS The **café** here, open daily 10–5, has sandwiches, snacks, and drinks to consume while watching BBC television on small screens. For a more filling choice, you won't have to go far. Nearly every shop from here to Oxford Circus is an eatery, including **Café Aroma** (273 Regent St., tel. 020/7495–4911), for sandwiches, coffee, and pastries; **Burger King** (298 Regent St., tel. 020/7924–3696); **McDonald's** (310 Regent St., tel. 020/7631–1561); and, one block over, **Efes** (175 Great Portland St., tel. 020/7436–0600), for a feast of kebabs and Turkish appetizers.

BEKONSCOT MODEL VILLAGE

This magical place all started with Roland Callingham's passion for making models in his garden. He built a model village that was (and is) a little slice of 1930s England, whereupon friends begged him to open it to the public. Seventy years later and now more than 2 acres, the world's oldest model village remains popular with children *and* grown-ups.

Even though there aren't many buttons to push—Bekonscot is all about old-fashioned charm—kids love discovering all that's hidden here, so take your time. (Meanwhile, you can marvel at the craftsmanship.) A work sheet helps kids hunt down items and points out details. If you follow the little marked pathway, you won't miss a thing.

Just about anything that can be is in miniature here, from a grimy colliery, where a conveyor belt brings chips of coal up from a mine, to a zoo, castle, church, pubs, and stately Hanton Court Maze, which has tiny hedges being clipped by a gardener. Notice that some names are tongue-in-cheek, such as Jerry Builder and Dan D. Lyon (the florist).

HEY, KIDS! For her eighth birthday treat, the young Queen Elizabeth visited Bekonscot. She tripped and cut her leg, and, so the story goes, a yellow antiseptic liquid was carefully dabbed on. The cut healed well, and soon after the event, the magically effective but vile-smelling, stinging liquid, known as TCP, received the royal warrant, probably the highest seal of approval a product can get in England.

 Warwick Rd., Beaconsfield.
Rail: Beaconsfield

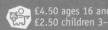 £4.50 ages 16 and up,
£2.50 children 3–15

 Mid-Feb–Oct, daily 10–5

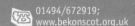 01494/672919;
www.bekonscot.org.uk

 3 and up

Kids tend to like the moving models best. You can watch for ages as little trains trundle through tunnels and stop at stations. Over a year they travel 16,000 miles around this tiny circuit. In the Maryloo signal box, a full-size human works the controls. At the harbor below, you'll see fish for sale, with dinky vegetables in the shop next door. If you can get on your knees and press your face against the Tudor leaded window of Splashynge Hall, you'll glimpse its tasteful furnishings. At the fairground, not a great deal has changed, as the Ferris wheel, chair swings, and other spinning, whizzing rides are still popular today.

A later addition to Bekonscot is a memorial miniature to children's author Enid Blyton, who lived at Beaconsfield for more than 30 years and whose works are as popular in Britain as Beatrix Potter's or Roald Dahl's. She is busy at her typewriter in the garden. And there goes Noddy, one of her characters, in his famous little yellow car—aaahhh.

KEEP IN MIND
This is not an activity for a wet day, as the model village and playground are outside. Bekonscot was not intended as a profit-making attraction, and it's still managed by the Church Army, an organization like the Salvation Army, which gives proceeds to needy causes.

EATS FOR KIDS Hot and cold snacks are available from the **kiosk.** In Beaconsfield village, a few minutes' walk away, the **Old White Swan** pub (London Rd., tel. 01494/673800) serves daily specials, such as chili and rice, spinach and mushroom lasagna, and Swan burgers (pure beef—no swan!). Children's meals include golden tiddlers (tiny fried fish shapes), chicken nuggets, sausages, and burgers. The homemade desserts are to die for, all served at old-world wooden booths.

BFI LONDON IMAX CINEMA

Space-age conservatory or grounded UFO? From the minute you see this huge cylindrical glass building with a color-splashed mural and foliage-covered tentacles, you know you're in for something special. The bright new building is the home of the British Film Institute's IMAX cinema, with the largest screen in the U.K. A trip to the movies here—whether you're seeing a 3-D show or a more traditional two-dimensional one—pulls you into the world on screen and provides an experience that's weird, fascinating, and thrilling.

The first tip-off to the size of the screen is that you take an elevator to reach your seat. Sitting at about mid-screen level, you can't help but feel like a dot on the landscape. When the show starts, sound blasts from every angle, and the high-tech visual effects make you feel like you're traveling back in time or across the world. Perhaps you'll wander the winding corridors of Egyptian pyramids and discover ancient mysteries, go on safari in the Serengeti and dodge a stampede of wildebeests, plunge to the depths of the sea and

KEEP IN MIND
After you see a movie, go see the real thing. Some of the films have been made with the help of other London institutions, such as the London Aquarium, for *Into the Deep,* and the British Museum, for *Mysteries of Egypt.*

EATS FOR KIDS
The spacious, glass-and-steel, ground-floor **café** is a great place to watch the world go round, through floor-to-ceiling windows that double as the curved walls of this cylindrical building. Snack on ices, scrumptious slices of chocolate fudge cake, carrot cake, pre-packed sandwiches, and potato chips, daily 11–8:45. Gabriel's Wharf and its selection of eateries (*see* HMS *Belfast*) is a brisk riverside walk away. Here you'll find **Studio Six** (tel. 020/7928–6243), a clapboard hut with a great evening buzz and fun food to match, including yummy fries. The moderately priced fare changes daily and includes pasta, grills, and fish cakes.

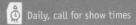

 South Bank, Waterloo, SE1.
Tube: Waterloo

 £6.75 ages 17 and up,
£4.75 children 5–16;
workshops free

Daily, call for show times

020/7902–1234, 020/7960–3120
workshops; www.bfi.org.uk

 6 and up

swim with sea lions, or blast into space and walk weightlessly beside astronauts on the moon.

Watching in 3-D may make you want to shrink back in your seat so that the images don't hit you between the eyes. (Those prone to motion sickness should beware.) For these films you wear a pair of dark plastic glasses that adjust images produced by two projection systems. If you remove the glasses, you get an idea of how it works. Without them, your eyes can only focus on one layer of images; the rest looks out of focus.

Kids' workshops during Easter and summer vacations (usually weekdays at 11:30) can add to the experience. Aimed at under-11s (accompanied by parents), workshops are tied to the current feature's theme and generally include an explanation of the magic of 3-D and a craft project. They're great for would-be animators, crafty types, and curious moviegoers alike.

HEY, KIDS! How huge is IMAX? The silver screen here is the biggest in Britain. It would take 90 London taxis parked next to one another to cover it and five double-decker buses stacked on top of each other to equal its height. Take a closer look at the screen's surface, and you'll see it's full of holes—millions of them. These allow the sound, emanating from 44 loudspeakers, to come through and surround the audience. The IMAX projector, larger and more powerful than a conventional one, weighs 4,200 pounds. Even the film reels are ginormous, weighing in at 191 pounds each.

BRASS RUBBING CENTRE

Bet you didn't know ancient churches could be interactive, but they can. Instead of just wandering around and looking at the tombs, you can go to St. Martin-in-the-Fields and create a brass rubbing, a peculiarly English hobby that took hold in Victorian times. Down in the bustling crypt, you'll find the Brass Rubbing Centre (along with a café, bookshop, historical souvenir shop, and gallery), where you can create a color image of an ancient knight, gracious lady, grizzly mythological beast, or intricate Celtic pattern. You can choose from more than a hundred images, including such famous kings and queens as Henry VIII, Charles I, and Elizabeth I.

The brasses on display are replicas of some of England and Europe's best engraved memorial plaques. (Replicas are used to preserve the originals, which were walked on and rubbed by enthusiasts for centuries.) These plaques were made for the well-to-do as early as the 11th century. (Notice the distinct Norman names, such as the noble-sounding Sir John D'Abernoun, from Surrey.) Plaques provided an eternal saintly image to which the living

EATS FOR KIDS To those Londoners in the know, the **Café in the Crypt** (tel. 020/7839–4342) is celebrated for its no-nonsense, budget-price menu, which changes daily. There are usually two hot meat or fish dishes (£5–£7) and a vegetarian option with proper homely English puds, aka pudding (around £2). All profits go back to the church, which sponsors an active homeless charity. Also see National Portrait Gallery.

St. Martin-in-the-Fields, Trafalgar Sq., WC2. Tube: Charing Cross, Leicester Sq.

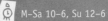

Free; image making £5 ages 13 and up, £4 children 12 and under

M–Sa 10–6, Su 12–6

020/7930–9306

7 and up

could pray and had the advantage of not taking up as much space as a bulky tomb. Take note of the changes in fashion, both in clothes and in armor. For instance, chain mail graduates to plate armor—for better protection against increasingly effective weapons.

After you decide which image to make, staff prepare your black or white paper, show you how to make an outline and the first gentle rub with special wax crayons, and how to correct your blips. It's easy once you get the hang of it. Allow at least 30–40 minutes to make a neat job. While kids are busy, mom and dad can wander around the church upstairs (designed by James Gibbs, a protégé of Sir Christopher Wren) or succumb to the temptation to rub as well.

HEY, KIDS! After you've completed your brass rubbing, see if you can read some of the worn tombstones on the floor of the crypt. One right by the concert information desk has a wonderful skull and crossbones in relief.

KEEP IN MIND Free lunchtime concerts are given at the church every Monday, Tuesday, and Friday, as is a regular (admission charged) evening program. Details are available in the crypt. After concerts and on Saturdays, the crypt gets really busy.

BRITISH AIRWAYS LONDON EYE

For the trip of the millennium (it opened January 2000) and an unrivaled bird's-eye view of London, climb aboard the world's largest observation Ferris-like wheel. During the 30-minute "flight," you gaze over the city near and far and, on a clear day, can see some 25 miles away.

The flight appeals to both young and old, and though from a distance (you can see it from most London bridges and high points) the Eye looks a little scary, don't worry. The 25-person observation capsules are so spacious and comfortable and travel so slowly (you barely sense it moving) that you shouldn't feel motion sickness or claustrophobia. (Fear of heights is a different story.) In fact, the Eye doesn't really stop, even as you embark, except for visitors in wheelchairs. Inside, you can stand, walk around, or sit on the central bench and view London in every direction.

A guide points out places of interest. To the west, Big Ben is a stone's throw across

EATS FOR KIDS The **Costa,** a café booth by the lineup area, sells light snacks and great coffee. Walk along the river to Gabriel's Wharf and its restaurants (see BFI London IMAX Cinema and HMS Belfast).

KEEP IN MIND Lines can be long—sometimes more than a 30-minute wait—on weekends and at peak vacation times. Tickets are sold on a timed basis, but even with a ticket, you'd be wise to show up 30 minutes before departure. You can call for advance tickets at least three days early (and then pick up your tickets the day of your trip) or purchase same-day or advance tickets in person from County Hall, adjacent to the Eye.

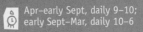

the river, along with the Houses of Parliament and what most kids call James Bond's headquarters: MI6, the government's secret service. Beyond is Nelson's Column, Buckingham Palace, and the Archbishop's Lambeth Palace, with its usually private gardens. To the east, you can see OXO Tower, Tate Modern, St. Paul's Cathedral, the Old Bailey law courts, the HMS *Belfast,* Canary Wharf, and the Millennium Dome. Farther south from Canary Wharf is Somerset House, the BT Tower, the green spaces of Hampstead Heath, and the spire of Highgate's village church. Other highlights include the radio mast of Crystal Palace, the twin towers of Wembley Stadium (until they're redesigned), and Windsor Castle. You can survey the curvy Thames and its many bridges, the many different colors of rooftops, and the usually private inner squares and courtyards.

Upon emerging from the wheel, you may want to go around again sometime. Next time try a magical nighttime flight or one at dusk. If you walk by the Eye then, you'll see myriad camera flasnes trying to capture the moment from the topmost capsules.

HEY, KIDS! Although the London Eye looks like a Ferris wheel (named after the U.S. engineer G. W. G. Ferris), it's much more than that. Ferris wheels are supported on both sides of the wheel, but this wheel, spectacularly overhanging the river, is supported by an A frame on just one side. Capsules are fixed to the outside of the wheel and are individually motorized to keep each one stable and upright.

BRITISH LIBRARY

This is not a library where you can check out the latest Harry Potter book (it's not a lending library at all but rather is used for reference and research), but you can discover some pretty magical things here. Take the building itself. It has a broad Mediterranean-type piazza entrance with an Anne Frank memorial tree, and inside, a light, white interior has staircases and escalators that lead to countless reading rooms. The library has a calming atmosphere, one that makes any child with an interest in reading want to investigate further.

In addition to books, journals, manuscripts, stamps, patents, sound recordings, printed music, and maps from recent centuries, this national library holds works from almost 3,000 years ago. The John Ritblat Gallery brings some of these treasures to the public eye in a permanent exhibition. You can listen to some weird and wonderful extracts from the National Sound Archives, including the voice of Florence Nightingale, an extract from the Beatles' last tour interview, and rare birdsong. On display are many letters on thick, worn paper in browned ink, including one written by Ghandi during his fast in 1943;

EATS FOR KIDS The first-floor **restaurant** has a hot dish of the day and a daily soup, plus a selection of sandwiches and pastries. As you munch, you can gaze at the rows upon rows of books in the King's Library (the library of King George III). A larger variety of sustenance is available at the popular deli **Goodfellas** (50 Lamb's Conduit St., tel. 020/7405–7088), where people line up for the upstairs buffet.

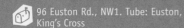
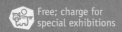

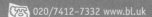
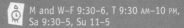
Nelson's last letter to his lover Emma, along with a lock of his hair; and one in secret cipher written by Charles I during the British Civil War. Writers' original folios represent Shakespeare, Tolstoy, Balzac, and Austen, and composers' tomes, several inches thick, include Handel and Bach—quite a contrast to the Beatles' color felt-tip scribblings on scraps of paper. Some sacred texts have only survived as fragments, on pieces of papyrus, cotton, and palm leaf. Though it's not possible to run your fingers over these thick old manuscripts, you can use Turning the Pages, a computer screen simulation that lets you leaf through books, such as Leonardo da Vinci's notes, page by page. Towering in the center of the building is a six-story glassed-in column that houses the library of King George III. It contains 65,000 books, mainly reference tomes—a fitting heart to this huge library with more than enough for even hardened bookworms.

KEEP IN MIND
The Workshop of Words, Sound and Images is an interactive gallery tracing the story of book production. Free demonstrations of book binding and calligraphy take place most Saturdays.

HEY, KIDS! The British Library used to take up a vast amount of space at the British Museum. Since everything that is published in the U.K. finds its way onto these shelves, about 2 miles of additional shelf space was needed each year. The solution was this new library, which opened in 1999. The hope is that it will have room for whatever expansion is necessary.

BRITISH MUSEUM

Walking through the towering colonnaded entrance of this exalted institution, you have the feeling you're entering a magnificent temple, and you're right. The British Museum is a vast shrine to objects from around the globe—so vast, in fact, that you can't navigate the whole collection at once. More noteworthy for kids than size, however, is that the museum has shaken off its musty image, yielding a bright, fresh experience.

Along with better shops and a restaurant in the new Great Court, the fresh kids'-eye view comes courtesy of the Young Visitors Centre, your first stop. Here you can get information about special events and pick up self-guided tours. Next, you might want to visit the renovated Reading Room, where you can surf the museum's collections. It's great for prioritizing your must-sees but no substitute for the real things in the galleries.

All kids love mummies—the Egyptian ones, that is. In the Roxie Walker Galleries, attractive displays bring the weird and wonderful rituals of this ancient civilization

KEEP IN MIND Because of the museum's huge size, allow at least two hours for a first visit. Sundays can be quite crowded and are best avoided. The new bookshop has a great selection of cards, books, gifts, and souvenirs, many of which are hard to find elsewhere.

EATS FOR KIDS At the **Great Court Café,** you can people-watch while munching on sandwiches and sticky patisserie. With repro Greek-battle wall friezes, the ground-floor **Restaurant & Café** serves changing hot meals and salads, including kids' options (often sausages and chicken nuggets), after noon, and sandwiches and snacks from 10 AM. Opposite the main entrance, **Pizza Express** (30 Coptic St., tel. 020/7636–3232) has a streamlined Italian bistro setting; the staff and choice of pizza, pasta, and salads are always spot on. Minimalist canteen-style **Wagamama** (4A Streatham St., tel. 020/7323–9223) serves economical soft noodle, dumpling, and rice dishes.

Great Russell St., WC1. Tube:
Holborn, Russell Sq., Tottenham Ct. Rd.

£2 suggested donation

Th–F 10–8:30, Sa–W 10–5:30

020/7323–8000;
www.british-museum.ac.uk

6 and up

to life (don't worry—not literally). You can see gilded and brightly painted cases, decorated urns, and fascinating daily objects, including toys that were intended for use in the next world. Imaging techniques let you actually see inside one mummy's wrappings to the bare bones, and you can learn about the gruesome but practical methods of preserving bodies.

The Greeks are worth a look, too; in the Parthenon Galleries you can see the Elgin Marbles, sculptures obtained from a site in ancient Athens. A debate about whether to return them to Greece has been rumbling for decades, so admire them while they're still here.

You can check out the tribes who first roamed England, including a good 1st-century example of Lindow Man, who was perfectly preserved in a peat bog. Close by is the Sutton Hoo haul of jewel-encrusted daggers, swords, and helmets, which adorned Redwald, King of the Angles during the 7th century. You can also browse the collection of exhibits on early North American people, including the feather headdress of Yellow Calf.

HEY, KIDS! The newest part of the museum is the awesome glass-and-steel-ceiling Great Court, which links the museum to the spectacular azure-and-gold domed Reading Room. Check out the amazing Great Court roof, which consists of 3,500 triangles of glass—enough for about 500 garden green-houses. If that doesn't seem like a lot to you, imagine what the Reading Room was once like. After it was built in the 1850s, the whole 2-acre public court-yard was taken over by miles of books, now housed in the British Library. That's a lot of books.

CABINET WAR ROOMS

58

During World War II, this warren of rooms below the government offices of Whitehall was the nerve center of the war operation. Winston Churchill, along with the most important people in the military and government, worked and slept in this secret bunker while the German Luftwaffe attacked the streets above. Today you can tour these historic rooms, some of which have been kept exactly as they were before the war ended. It's as if time stood still—literally. The clocks all read two minutes to five, and background sounds include wailing sirens, voices and footsteps in the corridors, and the tap-tap of busy typewriters. It makes for an eerie atmosphere but an informative visit.

A free audio guide explains both about the war business conducted in each room and about daily life. (Some of the anecdotes are really funny.) You can even see secret rooms that were off-limits to most of the war office staff, including the tiny room in which Churchill made frequent telephone calls to President Roosevelt. Because staff worked and slept in shifts around the clock, the manual typewriters had specially muffled keys to keep their

EATS FOR KIDS Since the secrecy of the war rooms cannot be compromised, no outside catering operations have been allowed entrance. You will be forced to conduct reconnaissance at an outside location. Head to the junction of Horse Guards Road and Birdcage Walk, and walk down Storey's Gate to the ornately decorated Central Hall (a former Methodist church), opposite Westminster Abbey. In the crypt, the budget-price **Wesley Café** (Storey's Gate, tel. 020/7222–8010) has a limited daily choice of hot and cold meals from £4.75. Also see Westminster Abbey.

 Clive Steps, King Charles St., SW1.
Tube: Westminster

 £5 ages 17 and up

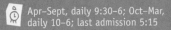 Apr–Sept, daily 9:30–6; Oct–Mar,
daily 10–6; last admission 5:15

020/7930–6961;
www.iwm.org.uk

 12 and up

incessant tapping from waking sleepers, especially Churchill. You also learn, for example, that it was very hard to be Churchill's secretary. He dictated directly to the typewriter, but his slight speech impediment and impatience could make typing for him more than a little difficult. You can read for yourself some of his many speeches, complete with his own handwritten corrections.

Indeed, Churchill is the most compelling subject here. You can see his constant props, cigars and whisky, and hear how during the Blitz, consumption went up considerably. You also learn that officials constantly suspected poisoning and that one solution was to try things out on the staff or dogs, who were more disposable than war leaders—just another aspect here that is at once haunting and interesting.

HEY, KIDS! On one occasion, the whisky decanter became mysteriously cloudy and so was sent for analysis in case it had been poisoned. Someone had added to it all right, but what they'd added was water. Some staff member must have taken some whisky and tried to cover up by diluting it back to the old level.

KEEP IN MIND Naturally, students of modern history and the war find this place fascinating, but so, too, do those who lived during the time—i.e., grandparents. Allow more than an hour to do the tour, plus some time to browse through the excellent books in the souvenir shop.

CHANGING OF THE GUARD

Photo collections of London are incomplete without a picture of one of the stone-face guards in his black bearskin hat and bright red tunic, with rifle shouldered. If you're in the right place at the right time, you can snap them in boot-stamping action as they change over at various royal locations. Buckingham Palace, the Queen's London home, is the premier location, but since other monarchs have held court elsewhere, you can also guard-spot at the Tower of London; Horse Guards, by the old Whitehall Palace (only the Banqueting House remains); and St. James's Palace, the present home of Prince Charles.

Buckingham Palace puts on the biggest show, with marching band music and guards on horseback wearing golden helmets with jaunty white or red plumes. You can follow the route the relieving guards take from Wellington Barracks, down Birdcage Walk by St. James's Park, finally coming to a halt outside the gates of Buckingham Palace. (As the guards march, look for different uniform types, such as Grenadier, Coldstream,

EATS FOR KIDS North of Green Park, a few minutes' walk away, the **Hard Rock Cafe** (150 Old Park La., tel. 020/ 7629–0382) bulges with rock memorabilia, plays loud music, and does a great business in burgers as well as kids' menus for under-10s.

HEY, KIDS! Can you imagine knights in armor jousting in the center of London? That's what happened at Horse Guards in 1540, when Henry VIII held a grand tournament for all the great knights of Europe. Just picture scenes from *Excalibur* and *First Knight* as you gaze upon the vast open tiltyard. And if you're wondering what tiltyard means, it's the place where "tilting" (also known as jousting) contests took place. In a tilt, a knight on horseback charged, thrust his lance, and tried to knock his opponent off his horse.

Buckingham Palace and Whitehall, SW1. Tube:
Victoria, St. James's Park

 020/7839–1377 Buckingham Palace, 020/
7414–2479 Household Division, 0891/505452
London Tourist Board recording (50p per min)

  Free

 Buckingham Palace Apr–early Sept,
daily 11:30, check for times in fall
and winter; Horse Guards daily 11, 4

All ages

and Scots.) It's a great sight, even bringing traffic to a stop. To get the best view at Buckingham Palace, go directly there (arriving at 11), and find a high spot on the Victoria Memorial statue, opposite the gates. To hear the shouted commands and get a closer look at the rifle switching, press your face against the railings and be prepared to get squashed in summer.

Horse Guards, once Henry VIII's tournament ground, is the setting for Trooping the Colour. On the second Saturday in June (her official birthday), the Queen rides from Buckingham Palace with her guard and salutes the precisely lined troops before returning to the palace. It's an amazing spectacle. You can try for tickets in advance by mail, including some for rehearsals the two previous Saturdays. If you chance it without tickets, you may only get a view of the horse's rear ends on the open side of the road. The mounted sentries of the Household Division perform their usual, slightly smaller-scale ceremony at Horse Guards daily.

KEEP IN MIND If you're in London in November, you can see the centuries-old procession of the Queen in the Irish State Coach with her guards, carrying out the ceremony of the Opening of Parliament. (Check with tourist information centers for the precise date.) Guard devotees should also visit the Guards Museum (Birdcage Walk, tel. 020/7930–4466), open daily 10–4, with a small admission charge.

CHESSINGTON WORLD OF ADVENTURES

I f your kids want their insides thrown out, or at least thoroughly shaken, then the rides at Chessington are for them. This adventure land, 25 miles southwest of London and easily reached from Waterloo station, is split into loosely themed zones: Pirate's Cove, Mystic East, Mexicana, Transylvania, Forbidden Kingdom, Market Square, Toytown, and the latest, Beanoland. Admission gets you onto all the main rides, but since the big thrills attract the longest lines, arrive early and plan well to cut waiting time. There's also a good selection of games and rides for younger adventurers.

Each ride has a thrillometer star rating, and most every kid rates Samurai (Mystic East) as terrifyingly tops. Encased in a seat on one of the arms, you hang on for dear life as you are spun around as if on a Japanese warrior's sword. If you survive, you might be game for the other breathtaking ride, Rameses Revenge (Forbidden Kingdom). This is the ultimate punishment for all those who have disturbed the mummies in the Forbidden Tomb, where explorers are treated to a jolly good drenching and a bit of spinning and twirling up high.

HEY, KIDS! Har-har! Chortle-chortle! Gnee-hee! You'll hear this and more on the rides in Beanoland, based on the children's comic strip *The Beano*, which has been a favorite in England for more than 50 years. None of that naughty kid magic, as devised by the British Dennis the Menace and his four-legged friend Gnasher, has been lost over the decades. Here's your chance to enjoy all the larger-than-life comic-strip characters through water splashing, dodgem (bumper) cars, splatting, and other wickedly fun activities.

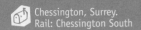
Chessington, Surrey.
Rail: Chessington South

0870/444-7777;
www.chessington.com

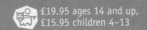
£19.95 ages 14 and up,
£15.95 children 4–13

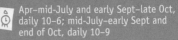
Apr–mid-July and early Sept–late Oct,
daily 10–6; mid-July–early Sept and
end of Oct, daily 10–9

3 and up

For those who'd rather warm up to the excitement before going on the biggies, the Black Buccaneer (Pirate's Cove) is ideal: a pirate ship swings back and forth until you are almost horizontal. If you want to get souped up, Vampire Run (Transylvania) and the Rattlesnake (Mexicana) should get pulses racing, and the Rodeo (Mexicana) makes you feel like you're losing your seat.

If you haven't the stomach for all this, or have younger kids in tow, head to Toytown's diversions. Elsewhere, at the popular Professor Burp's Bubbleworks, you are defied to emerge dry. The Sky Safari takes you over a large section of park, yielding great glimpses of the many wild and exotic animals. Paws and Claws includes meerkats, lions and tigers, gorillas, and enchanting sea lions, which give shows, as do the birds of prey. Just how much adventure can you fit into one day?

EATS FOR KIDS
Unless you take a picnic—though in this huge park, carrying extra baggage is a pain—you'll have to rely on one of the many hunger busters: **McDonald's, Pizza Hut, KFC, Mexican Diner,** and **Alpine Café.** Sweet treats can be nibbled on at the **Cadbury Castle.**

KEEP IN MIND Many of the larger, wilder rides have height restrictions for safety, ranging from minimums of 35 inches to 55 inches. On some rides, children must be accompanied by an adult: there's a list on the brochure you get as you enter. Chessington is part of the Tussaud's group, which offers a season-ticket scheme covering admission to other attractions, such as the London Planetarium, Madame Tussaud's, and Rock Circus (see listings for each).

COURTAULD GALLERY

When it comes to art museums, small is beautiful, especially with children. The small size of this gallery is its chief asset, making it easy to navigate and manageable for kids, and the setting and paintings provide a visual feast.

The prettiest approach to the gallery is from the river, by the steps on Waterloo Bridge, and past the recently renovated buildings that make up the whole of Somerset House (*see below*). The gallery entrance is across the cobbled courtyard.

The gallery rooms were the first home, from 1780, of the Royal Academy of Arts, which later moved to Burlington House, in Piccadilly, in 1837. If you look up at the decorative plasterwork ceilings, you can still see the curly RA initials. The rooms have had a recent makeover, but the main reason for coming here is to see monumental works by world-famous Impressionists and Post-Impressionists.

EATS FOR KIDS See Somerset House (*see below*). A short walk away, the ultimate family entertainment restaurant, **Smolensky's** (105 Strand, tel. 020/7497-2101), has games and magicians. The Tex-Mex-oriented food doesn't quite match up to the class of the Art Deco interior, but kids have a ball.

KEEP IN MIND You can also plunge your kids into the world of painting through free drop-in workshops the first Saturday of each month (11–1). These mini master classes allow children to look more closely at a particular artist or style and then produce their own masterpieces—perhaps pastel drawings influenced by Renoir or fabric-pen designs created after looking for textile patterns in paintings. In addition to enriching a young mind, you can save money, as one adult per child is admitted free. Separate workshop events during the holidays, for different ages, cost £10–£15 and last four or more hours.

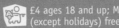
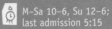

In order to help kids get the most out of the Courtauld (and yet still enjoy the collection yourself), arm yourselves with a children's gallery-trail booklet at the admission desk. These free self-guiding quizzes—best for ages 6–12—turn out to be fun for parents, too. Covering the gallery's key paintings and giving a neat art-history tour, the "Different Kinds of Painting" booklet begins at the beginning. Albertinelli's *The Creation and Fall,* an early narrative painting almost 500 years old, spotlights the story of Adam and Eve. The quiz trail then romps through another 100 years to the genius of the Dutch old masters and their portraits and landscapes, before leaping to Impressionists, just over 100 years ago, and *A Bar at the Folies-Bergère* by Manet. It's a whistle-stop tour of different art styles.

If you'd rather go straight to the Impressionist gems, head up the winding marble staircase. From Monet's *Autumn Effect at Argenteuil* to *The Haystacks,* by Gauguin, an interested child can spend ages filling out "A Painting for Every Season," another kids' booklet. It's not unusual to find yourself stepping over children sprawled on the floor drawing intently.

HEY, KIDS! The name "Impressionists" was not originally meant to be a compliment. By calling the new style of paintings "impressions," late-19th-century critics were actually mocking them, considering them to be rough and unfinished works rather than proper images. Turning the tables, struggling artists adopted the name for themselves, and the rest is history. Today these "sketchy" paintings, rejected for decades, are now admired around the globe, and many sell for millions.

COVENT GARDEN

High-fashion shops, craft stalls, restaurants, entertainment, and some of the best free street shows around—Covent Garden has it all. From its epicenter—the cobbled piazza and its market—to the surrounding streets, packed with trendy shops and eateries, it's hard to picture the medieval monks who once tended the "convent garden" for Westminster Abbey here. Produce markets sprouted over the centuries, but it was the Victorians who built the steel-and-glass market halls. Although the Central Market Hall has been restored, the halls bordering the piazza, Jubilee Hall (selling crafts) and the London Transport Museum, are original.

The only building remaining from the square's original 17th-century Italianate design, however, is St. Paul's, the actors' church, whose walls are dotted with great performers' plaques (look for Charlie Chaplin's). In front is *the* street theater hot spot, where mimes line the route to the tube station. Some are painted in one color and hold a pose for minutes until a passerby catches their glassy stare and cues the routine. Around the piazza, musicians

EATS FOR KIDS Escape the hordes at **Mela** (152–156 Shaftesbury Ave., tel. 020/7836–8635), a bright, modern, Indian restaurant where the food is cooked before your eyes. Choose from flat breads and pancakes (*naan, paratha, dosai*) to roll with spiced vegetables, chicken, and fish, starting at £1.95. The **Vilar Floral Hall Café** (Royal Opera House) is high on spectacle and prices, offering cakes and pastries, sandwiches and salads. The Central Market Hall is cheaper; catch the shopping and entertainment buzz while feasting on huge sandwiches and stuffed potatoes at **Ponti's** (Unit 4, The Market, tel. 020/7836–1662). Also see the London Transport Museum and Theatre Museum.

Covent Garden Piazza and Central Market, WC2. Tube: Covent Garden

 Free

 Piazza daily 24 hrs; Jubilee Market Hall M 9–3, T–Su 9–5; Central Market Hall daily 10–5, some shops and restaurants much later

 020/7836–9136 Covent Garden Central Market

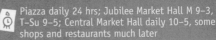 All ages

range from Chinese players with twangy, melodious strings and exotic box instruments to bouncy Peruvian groups in Andean costume. In the central covered market by the downstairs terrace cafés, a sultry pair might dance the tango.

The Royal Opera House, home to the Royal Ballet, has gotten a massive makeover. The grand old entrance is still on Bow Street, but a new entrance opens on the piazza. Step inside and enjoy the new spaces, particularly the restored Floral Hall, formerly a storeroom and, before that, a 19th-century market selling flowers. Now it's a public area where you can get snacks, gaze up at the high glass ceiling, and admire displays of old spangled ballet costumes, including some worn by Margot Fonteyn. An escalator takes you to the Vilar Floral Hall Bar and an outdoor balcony with a magnificent view across the market rooftops to Nelson's Column and the tourists and pigeons in Trafalgar Square. Dancers' rehearsal rooms have windows onto the balcony; if you're lucky, you might glimpse a young star.

KEEP IN MIND
The London Transport Museum and Theatre Museum (see below) are next to the piazza. Across Long Acre, and to the left of Neal Street, is Neal's Yard, a mock rustic courtyard with whole-food shops and eating places and a quirky water clock that performs hourly.

HEY, KIDS! Street theater, including puppetry, has been a tradition here for centuries. In 1662, the great diarist Samuel Pepys noted that he had enjoyed an Italian puppet play here—the best he ever saw, and probably the first Mr. Punch show. For over 25 years, the annual May Fayre (tel. 020/7287–0907) has celebrated this theatrical event in the garden of St. Paul's, where over 30 gaily striped Punch-and-Judy booths stage performances on the second Sunday in May. It's wonderful free entertainment and a great chance to enjoy a British seaside and fairground tradition. There's puppet making for kids, too.

CUTTY SARK

Walk the decks of this beautiful ship, and you'll be taking a step into the past. The last of the clippers that sailed the seas to bring back tea and spices from China, she is resplendent with masts and rigging and is one of the London riverside's most famous historic sights. As you board, breathe in a little of the smoky aroma of Lapsang souchong tea absorbed over the years.

The history of the ship, launched in 1869, is told in storyboards, with captions especially for kids at the base of each board. In its glory days, the *Cutty Sark* (Scots for "cut short") sliced through the seas and set record journey times to the other side of the world. When her cargo changed from tea to wool and thus her route from China to South Australia, she could dash off the voyage in just 77 days, overtaking the mail steamship.

On the deck below, find out if you pass muster as a sailor by pulling some of the weighted blocks and tackles for hoisting the sails, but first feel the strength of the sail section

KEEP IN MIND

Wear sensible shoes as there are steep, narrow steps to negotiate. If you're planning to visit the three main Greenwich maritime sights—the *Cutty Sark,* National Maritime Museum, and Royal Observatory (*see below*)—get a Passport Ticket (£12 adults, a savings of £5).

EATS FOR KIDS

Follow the seafaring theme at the 18th-century **Trafalgar Tavern** (Park Row, tel. 020/8858–2437), in whose paneled rooms Charles Dickens used to be a regular. The specialty is whitebait (a tiny white fish), which was once caught locally. Government ministers used to travel downriver from Westminster to feast on it. Children's options include bangers and mash (sausage and mashed potatoes), fish sticks, and chicken nuggets. In Greenwich village, burger restaurants include **Café Rouge** (30 Stockwell St., tel. 020/8293–6660), at the French-style burger and fries end. Also see Greenwich Park, National Maritime Museum, and Royal Observatory.

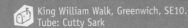 King William Walk, Greenwich, SE10.
Tube: Cutty Sark

 £3.50 ages 16 and up,
£2.50 children 5–15

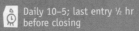 Daily 10–5; last entry ½ hr
before closing

 020/8858-3445;
www.cuttysark.org.uk

 4 and up

by the stairs. Then imagine it being wet from storm and spray, increasing its weight many times over. Rope knotting was a necessary skill. It's amazing how many types there are to learn, each with a purpose. (On weekends and in summer, there are knot demonstrations by a real salty dog sailor.) To rest your weary bones, try getting in a hammock, but mind your balance lest you fall.

Above deck, officers' and crew accommodations have been restored to their original condition—all shiny wood and authentic fittings. The captain's saloon is the most luxurious; note the hanging tray that holds wineglasses secure. For the rest of the crew, accommodations are spare, as you can see by peering in on some of the waxwork crew at ease in their quarters. Above deck is the wonderful web of rigging, totaling 11 miles—such a romantic sight when set against the towers of the city in the distance.

HEY, KIDS! Captain Woodget was one of the *Cutty Sark*'s most celebrated captains, respected by all who worked with him (and it was a tough job). To lighten up a little, he used to ride his bicycle on deck with his three dogs following behind. Check out the photo of him and his beloved pets in the exhibit on the ship's history.

DOCKLANDS

Look at any London map, and you'll see the snaking Thames, which turned the city into a thriving port beginning with the Romans in 55 BC. But World War II's air raids changed that; the docks were bombed, river trade began a downturn, and the landscape from Tower Bridge to Canary Wharf on the Isle of Dogs grew ugly. Recently, however, the area has been regenerated with water-sport and leisure centers, office buildings, and wharfside loft apartments, while leaving plenty of the old to uncover. Among the dockside buildings, pubs, and ferry steps, you can find fascinating nooks and crannies with tales to tell.

Start in the picturesque haven of St. Katharine's Dock, in the shadow of Tower Bridge. Here the Dickens Inn brewery is just one of the old buildings at the water's edge. Meander around the luxury yachts and rustic barges, and exit the dock for the Thames Path, on the riverside. This small section of a 50-mile walkway emanating from the river's source provides almost a microhistory of London. Venturing into the next neighborhood, Wapping, reveals pirate history—from Wapping Stairs, where convicted pirates were put to death, to the Town of

KEEP IN MIND The Docklands Visitor Centre (3 Limeharbour, Tube: Crossharbour, tel. 020/7512–1111) furnishes free maps and area information, including a video and small local-history exhibit. The Docklands Museum (Unit C14, Poplar Business Park, 10 Prestons Rd., tel. 020/7515–1162), opening September 2001, contains interactives and a children's gallery.

St. Katharine's Dock, Tower Bridge, E1, to Island Gardens, Isle of Dogs, E14. Tube: Tower Gateway

 Free

 Daily 24 hrs

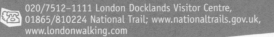
020/7512–1111 London Docklands Visitor Centre, 01865/810224 National Trail; www.nationaltrails.gov.uk, www.londonwalking.com

 All ages

Ramsgate pub (*see below*), where Judge Jeffreys, who sealed the pirates' fate, was himself clapped in irons. Captain Blood, who tried to steal the Crown Jewels from the Tower of London, was also captured here. Other preserved dockside buildings, which once stored tea and spices from India, make a grand sight.

For the intrepid, the path continues through several more docks (about 4 miles) to the Isle of Dogs, the heart of modern Docklands. To save energy, take the Docklands Light Railway from Tower Gateway to Island Gardens, at the tip of the Isle of Dogs peninsula. The elevated railway passes towering state-of-the-art buildings on numerous quaysides. One of the high points, literally, is at Canary Wharf, where No. 1, Canada Square, Britain's tallest building, looms overhead. While at Island Gardens, admire the view that Canaletto painted of the Queen's House and Royal Naval College across the river; it's timeless.

HEY, KIDS! Pirates were the scourge of the Thames, and so punishment for piracy was gruesome. At Wapping Old Stairs, by the romantically named Waterside Gardens, pirates were hanged to death, then tied to a stake at the foot of the steps, where the tide would wash over them. The notorious Captain Kidd, naval officer–turned–pirate, suffered this nasty fate in 1701.

EATS FOR KIDS Pubs are mainstays along the Thames Path. The popular **Prospect of Whitby** (57 Wapping Wall, tel. 020/7481–1095) serves good bar meals, including roasts and salads. The **Town of Ramsgate** (62 Wapping High St., tel. 020/7488–2685) still has an old-London fishing feel and a good daily menu, plus filled baked potatoes, pizza, ploughman's lunch (bread, cheese, salad), and sausage and mash (potatoes mashed with butter). Also see Thames Barrier Visitor Centre.

GOLDEN HINDE

Get on board me hearties! After circumnavigating the world and sailing more than 140,000 miles, the *Golden Hinde* has come to rest along the Thames. The galleon here is not the famous 16th-century man-of-war captained by Sir Francis Drake, however. That one rotted long ago. Instead, a beautiful handcrafted replica, docked between Southwark Cathedral and Shakespeare's Globe, acts as a living museum. When at sea, its small crew lives exactly as Drake's men did. Life was hard, and the men were tough, as you'll discover on this virtual voyage into the past.

On a self-guided tour, an information sheet details the parts of the ship and helps you sort out the mizzen from the main and fore masts. Better still is a tour with guides in period dress (book ahead). Either way, between the masts and the bowels of the ship, you can explore five decks. The poop deck, for instance, held the only private cabin—the captain's. (The crew slept among pigs, chickens, and sheep, which were kept for food.) In the main deck's armory, you can try turning the capstan to haul the anchor. On the

EATS FOR KIDS You need go no farther than the **Old Thameside Inn** (St. Mary Overy Dock, tel. 020/7403–4243), opposite the ship, for lunchtime sandwiches and salads. Actually a converted dock warehouse, it offers views over the river that can't be beat.

KEEP IN MIND The *Golden Hinde* is run by a small outfit, which survives on admission fees, so you may have to be patient when reserving a tour. You can also book a living-history night, during which your family (adults must accompany children) can dress, sleep, eat, and work as part of Drake's crew. It's an unforgettable experience. If you can't stay for the night, you might want to try one of the daytime summer workshops, offered when school is out. Call for details.

St Mary Overy Dock, Cathedral St., SE1.
Tube: London Bridge

 £9.50 ages 15 and up,
£6.50 children 4–14

 0870/0118700;
www.goldenhinde.co.uk

 Daily; times vary

6 and up

gun deck (painted red to camouflage bloodstains), you may get a chance to load the cannon and see it fire. By the way, if a lowly shipmate was found somewhere he shouldn't be, punishment was severe. If he stole food, for example, his hand would be nailed to the mast; after a few hours, the hand would probably have to be chopped off. "Luckily," among Drake's crew of musicians, cook, blacksmith, and minister, there was a barber surgeon, who performed amputations with only alcohol as painkiller.

Watch your head while descending the ladders to the lower decks; headroom is minimal to keep the boat's center of gravity low. Here you'll find the bilge, where rocks stabilized the ship; food-storage barrels; and the galley, where meals—including salted and dried beef, beans, prunes, currants, and sea biscuits, often with maggots and other creepy crawlies—were prepared. Food for thought: with all this, how were Drake's men so victorious in battle?

HEY, KIDS! Young boys on the crew worked hard. One of their tasks was to carry the gunpowder for the guns. The boys were called powder monkeys because they climbed up and down the ladders from the lower deck to the gun deck as fast as their bent, monkeylike legs could carry them. When off duty, powder monkeys slept on the deck floor (with mouths shut to prevent animal waste from sloshing into their mouths!) in the same set of ragged clothes.

GREENWICH PARK

Flanked by the river, Britain's largest royal park has been favored by kings and queens for centuries. Henry VIII hunted in the 183-acre park, and he and his two daughters, Mary I and Elizabeth I, were born here, in a palace that is no longer. In its place stands the Royal Naval Hospital buildings, now the National Maritime Museum (*see below*). At Elizabeth's Oak, the queen took tea in a hollow tree almost 6 feet across, which later became a prison for people who broke park rules. Earlier still, the park was the site of a Roman temple, whose remains you can see beyond Lover's Walk. But there are plenty of today's treasures to discover, too.

Of the park's beautiful panoramas, the best—looking across to St Paul's Cathedral on a clear day—is from the highest point, by the Royal Observatory (*see below*). The observatory is home to the Greenwich Meridian, and standing with your feet astride this famous line is de rigueur. If you don't visit the observatory, you can still span the hemispheres where the meridian crosses the avenue, leading to the observatory. Luckily, cars aren't allowed

EATS FOR KIDS There are many cafés in the park, but the most popular is the **Park Café** (Great Cross Ave., tel. 020/8858–9695), by the Royal Observatory. Sit at the outdoor tables, and order breakfast (all day), burgers, or baked potatoes with toppings. Another **Park Café** (St. Mary's Lodge, tel. 020/8293–0703) is inside the visitor center near the *Cutty Sark* and so is a practical place to get oriented. Inside the entrance, staff provide help, backed up by computer touch screens that highlight the history and culture of Greenwich. Also see *Cutty Sark*, National Maritime Museum, and Royal Observatory.

 King William Walk, Greenwich, SE10.
Tube: Cutty Sark

 Free

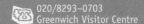 020/8293-0703
Greenwich Visitor Centre

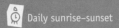 Daily sunrise–sunset

 All ages

on this road between 10 and 4, so you can take photos in safety. The hill here is great for rolling, running, or (in snow) sledding down.

Pretty walks lead to various gardens. The Flower Garden by the lake is a riot of color, scents, and butterflies in spring and summer. In spring, the Dell is magical; finches dart in and out of rhododendrons, and kids take cover, too, while playing hide-and-seek. If you are very quiet at the Wilderness, you may spot the shy deer that have lived and bred at Greenwich Park for centuries. For kids who'd rather jump, climb, and make loads of noise, a playground has enough apparatus to keep them happy for an hour or more.

To cap off a visit here, arrive by boat from Westminster in ancient maritime fashion. Allow about an hour for the journey.

HEY, KIDS! The red ball on top of the observatory has a very important job. It drops down its rod at 1 PM each day (and has since 1833), so sailors on the river can set their watches and clocks to Greenwich Mean Time.

KEEP IN MIND If you don't come by boat, come by tunnel. (But first, take a long look at the classic white maritime buildings from the North Bank—Canaletto, who painted it, liked the view, too.) Built in 1902 to replace a nearly 300-year-old ferry, the foot tunnel extends from Island Gardens, on the North Bank, to Greenwich, near the *Cutty Sark*. At its maximum depth it is 53 feet beneath the river, and the length is just under ¼ mile. It echoes eerily, but the atmosphere is really fun.

HAMPSTEAD HEATH

Covering almost 800 acres high above London, Hampstead Heath is a marvelous natural space flanked by two pretty villages, Hampstead, to the west, and Highgate, on the east. You can walk, admire the views, jog, picnic, cycle, rollerblade, float model boats, fly kites, climb trees and playground equipment, swim in ponds, and investigate a nature center here—all for free.

From Hampstead tube station, walk past the pretty shops and houses of Heath Street to Whitestone Pond, whose name comes from an old white milestone. Turn right on Spaniards Road, where on a clear day you can see London's prominent landmarks. Twice a year, around Easter and summer bank holidays, this footpath (which leads down to East Heath) resounds with the music and screams of a fair, here since the late-19th century, when the heath became free public land. At the foot of the East Heath section, Hampstead Ponds are filled with ducks and, in summer, bathers. You'll need to be a good swimmer and not mind mud and creepy crawlies between your toes, or just watch for waterfowl and, in

HEY, KIDS!
Kite Hill is really called Parliament Hill, because it was from here that Guy Fawkes and his gang, who tried to blow up Parliament in 1605, hoped to view their handiwork. Though their attempt was foiled, their plot is celebrated with fireworks every November 5th.

EATS FOR KIDS Hampstead village has a good selection of chain restaurants, from pizzerias to burger joints, but the heath pubs have more history. The **Freemasons Arms** (32 Downshire Hill, tel. 020/7433–6811) has leather chairs, a log fire, and traditional Sunday roasts. Also good for lunch is **Jack Straw's Castle** (North End Way, tel. 020/7435–8885), an old coaching inn named after the rebel peasant leader who hid here. It was also one of Charles Dickens's many watering holes. Sadly, the interior has been redone, but the location, perched on the edge of Whitestone Pond and the heath, is still great.

Hampstead, NW3; nature center
and pool: Gordon House Rd., NW5.
Tube: Hampstead

020/7482-7073
nature center

Free; pool £3.50 ages 17
and up, £1.50 children 10–16

Heath daily 24 hrs.; nature center Mar–Oct,
W–F 1–5, Sa–Su 10–5; Nov–Feb, W–F 1–4,
Sa–Su 10–4; pool May–Sept, daily 7–7

All ages

summer, dragonflies dancing above the water plants. Seasoned, year-round swimmers head to the west side of the heath towards Highgate Ponds, where there are segregated ponds for men and women (and one with serious model powerboats).

If you've come to fly a kite, you'll be in good company; Kite Hill is off to the left before Hampstead Ponds. At the heath's southernmost tip (around an hour's gentle walk from Whitestone Pond), a nature center teaches about the heath's history and wildlife through a little exhibit and computer program. Beside the nature center is the Lido, an outdoor swimming pool; a free mini-Lido (for kids under 10) is at the traditional playground at the foot of Kite Hill. Older kids prefer the jungle-style adventure playground a little farther on. After circumnavigating the heath, you'll probably be ready for rest and refreshment. Follow the footpath to the end, at the foot of Hampstead Ponds, and adjourn to Hampstead village and its many culinary delights.

KEEP IN MIND The suggested route covers a small section of the heath, skirting East Heath and Parliament Hill, north and east of Hampstead village, although even this could take a meandering three hours. To see another beautiful part of the heath, near Highgate, visit the area around Kenwood House (see below). If you have kids with limited stamina, visit the heath in microcosm at Golders Hill Park. There's a playground, bandstand, and animal enclosure with deer and goats, and an aviary with flamingoes and other birds— all free. A bit north of Hampstead proper, Golders Green is the nearest tube.

HAMPTON COURT

A long with wives, King Henry VIII couldn't resist collecting palaces, of which Hampton Court was the most magnificent. Sitting beside the Thames and surrounded by acres of parkland, it's a wonderful place to see and explore. Taking a boat from Richmond makes for a panoramic way to arrive, but it takes almost two hours. You'll need at least four hours to get the most of a visit here.

The vast palace contains royal apartments filled with 300 years of treasures. Standing in the cobbled courtyard entrance, you are catapulted back to the 1700s, as gentlemen of King William's court, dressed in a dandy's lacy finery, are ready to escort you on a guided tour. Tours are both fascinating and free. If you opt against one, look for a range of quiz sheets that form an investigative trail, especially good for children 11 and under.

Of all the rooms, the most absorbing are the Tudor Kitchens. But this food tour is not for everyone's palate ("gross" is the usual response). The butcher's room has splattered blood

EATS FOR KIDS The **Tiltyard Restaurant,** set among the rose and herbaceous gardens, has a wide-ranging menu of hot and cold food and kids' lunch boxes for around £3. You are welcome to eat in the outdoor patio and to bring your own picnic, which you can eat in the Wilderness area but not the formal gardens. If you don't bring your own food, you can pick something up at the grocery stores in nearby Hampton village.

East Molesey, Surrey.
Rail: Hampton Court

020/8781-9500;
www.hrp.org.co.uk

£10.50 ages 16 and up, £8.30 students,
£7 children 5–15; maze £2.30 ages 16
and up, £1.50 children; grounds free

Mid-Mar–mid-Oct, M 10:15–6, T–Su
9:30–6; mid-Oct–mid-Mar, daily 9:30–
4:30; last entry 45 mins before closing

5 and up

and holly sprigs for cleaning the tables. You can peer into the hanging room with swan, peacock, and boar; crush sage with mortar and pestle; and try lifting the massive pots, pans, and implements. Tables are laid with replicas, such as fish and deer pies, and baskets of real nuts and herbs to touch and smell. Over the roaring fire, a cauldron bubbles with soup, which you may be able to taste. Note the stool where a young boy would turn a spit with pig or boar. Feasting was serious stuff, and cooking was a hot, labor-intensive business.

There are over 60 acres of beautiful park and gardens around the palace. Children run around fountains and play in the Wilderness section, which includes Hampton Court's treasure: a magnificent hedged maze covering nearly a third of an acre. Children love wandering back and forth, hitting the same dead ends time and again. Wise parents sit outside, listen to their kids' delighted screams of frustration, and enjoy the tranquility of the gardens.

HEY, KIDS! Henry VIII didn't have Hampton Court built; he basically stole it. Its previous owner, Cardinal Wolsey, was becoming a little too big for his boots, and Henry wanted the palace for himself. So on the pretext of using it for a grand meeting that lasted a long time, Henry took it over and simply didn't hand it back.

KEEP IN MIND Throughout the year, there are special free programs, including little dramas. You might be asked to take part, perhaps joining in some Tudor dancing. There are also behind-the-scenes garden tours (separate charge). Ask at the Information Centre in the Clock Court, or phone ahead.

HAWK CONSERVANCY

Come by train (just over an hour from Waterloo) or by car (via the M3 and A303), but come. Even those with only a passing interest in raptors (birds of prey) will leave charmed and very much the wiser. You'll see birds native to the British Isles and from as far away as South America (most in captive breeding programs), from large condors to the small pygmy owl. You'll learn the difference between eagles, falcons, and hawks, and you might even develop a sneaking respect for vultures, those bottom-of-the-heap, bad-boy-image birds. Most birds are viewed in caged natural settings amid a small wooded park area surrounded by unspoiled woodland, but when the raptors come out to play, watch out.

Three daily demonstrations display the birds' talents. At the top flying field (large bird displays), you may want to duck as kites swoop from every direction, niftily catching food in flight. Meanwhile, a keeper tells all you need to know about these graceful flyers and happily answers questions almost endlessly afterwards. (The conservancy was started

KEEP IN MIND Make sure to arrive before noon, when the first of the major flying displays takes place, followed by others at 2 and 3:30. The displays, along with most of the attractions, are in the open air, so don't forget to bring cover for rain showers.

HEY, KIDS! Not all the birds at the conservancy are captive. At the sound of a bell each afternoon at the wildflower meadow, many beautiful wild birds—herons and some-times kites and other raptors that have been released back into the wild—come to feed. You can watch this wonderful scene undercover in the bird blind—but hush, or you'll scare them away.

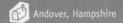 Andover, Hampshire

 01264/773850 voice,
01264/772252 recording;
www.hawk-conservancy.org

£5.75 ages 16 and up,
£3.25 children 3–15

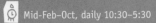 Mid-Feb–Oct, daily 10:30–5:30

 5 and up

by a nature-loving husband-and-wife team, and that caring family atmosphere is still very much in evidence.) The lower flying field features the fun and games of Chestnut, the tawny owl, and a mischievous kestrel. Undoubtedly, the most thrilling display is at the Valley of the Eagles, where three majestic bald eagles fly from a far field—you can just make them out as specks in the distance—to the display area, perfectly in time to dramatic music.

Between demonstrations, try wearing a special glove, steadying your nerves, and launching a Harris hawk into flight—not as easy as it looks. Stop along the leafy walkways and gaze at countless beautiful birds, particularly the elegant secretary bird and the many cute, wide-eyed owls. Don't forget to say a special hello to Duffy the eagle owl, with perky feathered ears; he's been around so long he practically owns the place. And why not place bets on the furry but feather-free ferrets, who run riot to raise funds for the hawk hospital?

EATS FOR KIDS The conservancy is deep in the countryside, so unless you have brought a picnic, you'll have to eat at **Duffy's,** named for you know whom. It serves a range of child-friendly meals and snacks, such as sausages, burgers, and fries, but not a raw chicken leg in sight, as these treats are reserved for the raptors.

HMS BELFAST

We don't mean to be sexist, but young boys just love clambering over the big guns on this warship, launched in 1938 and today Europe's last World War II survivor. In a fantastic location—on the Thames, in the shadow of the Tower of London—it provides an opportunity for kids to look at and learn about that period of history and about life on board ship. You'll find masses of items to look at, from gun shells to ship's rations, and a variety of informative videos, so allow up to two hours.

The ship is divided into eight zones, described on the self-guiding map on your entry ticket. Kids can take their own self-guided trail, whereby they're launched on an important mission. Following the captain's instructions, they are put to work, and after watching a video on how guns work, they are tested on paper. Upon successfully completing the assignment, they become honorary members of the ship's company. School vacations bring still more quiz trails and the occasional interactive drama.

EATS FOR KIDS The onboard **Walrus Café** is so called because of the tiny Walrus seaplanes that used to be stored here. Kids can admire the rivet- and pipe-lined walls while digging into a children's lunch box of sandwich, fruit, muffin, and drink (£4.50). Hearty dishes for young sailors include chicken drumsticks with baked beans, with more sophisticated chicken dishes for parents in charge. A short walk away toward Waterloo, Gabriel's Wharf has a larger selection of eateries, including the **Gourmet Pizza Company** (tel. 020/7928–3188). Wonderful pizza variations are big on toppings, and a boardwalk patio overlooks the river.

Morgan's Lane, Tooley St., SE1. Tube: London Bridge

 £5 ages 17 and up

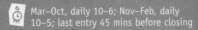 Mar–Oct, daily 10–6; Nov–Feb, daily 10–5; last entry 45 mins before closing

020/7940–6300; www.hmsbelfast.org.uk, www.iwm.org.uk

 5 and up

Apart from the guns, the captain's bridge is a definite hot spot. Here you get a taste of what it was like to command this huge vessel in a red alert. Lifelike models and frenetic voice recordings re-create what the crew of the *Belfast* encountered against the German battle cruiser *Scharnhorst* (one of the enemy's largest warships) at the Battle of North Cape. The boiler and engine rooms down below are massive, necessary to drive this great warhorse, which, at full steam, ran at 80,000 horsepower. On other decks, you'll learn about the hard life of an ordinary seamen, rum rations notwithstanding. (While serving for two years in the Far East, the crew washed down 56,000 pints of Navy rum.)

KEEP IN MIND
The many different decks are linked by steep ladderlike stairs, so it's a good idea to wear comfortable, stable shoes with non-slip soles. Sneakers are ideal.

Augmenting the experience, videos show reenactments of the ship's heroic engagements, explain how important areas of the ship worked, and demonstrate what had to be done to make the ship watertight if a shell hit.

HEY, KIDS! Each of the HMS *Belfast*'s triple, 175-ton guns had a range of 14 miles. Currently the turrets are trained on a service station on the M1 motorway. So watch out you road ragers; you're in the line of fire!

IMPERIAL WAR MUSEUM

A pair of big guns guarding the main entrance might make you think this massive museum is merely a glorified showcase for war making. It's much more than that, however. In addition to housing exhibits on 20th-century war tactics and machinery, it chronicles the personal side of wartime—terror, bravery, and the spirit of camaraderie.

Among the impressive hardware here are howitzers, a Sherman tank, German one-man submarine, and armored cars. Air weapons include a Lancaster bomber, V2 rocket, and a bomber you can get inside. You can also look through a huge periscope that can focus as far as St Paul's Cathedral.

But there are also exhibits on life during wartime. Away from the front lines, the focus is on women's fashions and food, and poetry and art reveal emotion in the heat of battle. The Blitz Experience gives a taste of London during the German air bombardment of World War II. In a reconstructed air-raid shelter on a 1940 street, you smell acrid smoke;

HEY, KIDS!
In wartime Britain, food was rationed. Can you imagine having to eat powdered everything, from milk to eggs, and margarine in tins? You were allowed just a handful of sweets and very few goodies each week. Check out a typical weekly grocery ration in the Home Front, in the World War II section.

KEEP IN MIND Museum areas on concentration camps can be distressing for younger children, as can a major new permanent Holocaust exhibition, which charts this tragic episode in great detail. Kids who are keen on learning about the uniforms and battles of earlier centuries should march around to the National Army Museum (Royal Hospital Rd., Chelsea, tel. 020/7730–0717).

Lambeth Rd., SE1. Tube: Elephant and
Castle, Lambeth North

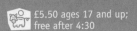 £5.50 ages 17 and up;
free after 4:30

 Daily 10–6

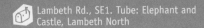 020/7416–5000; www.iwm.org.uk

 6 and up

hear sirens, fire-engine bells, and the bombs themselves; and imagine fearing whether your home was destroyed. The Trench, a reconstruction of the Somme, France, in 1916, shows the ghastliness of World War I trench warfare. Lighting, sounds, and smells re-create what a "tommy" soldier endured, from trench foot (rot from constantly standing in mud and water) to the horror of climbing out of the trench into a barrage of gunfire.

The role of secrets is touched upon, too. On the ground floor you can try to decipher some Morse code, while on the first floor, an espionage and intelligence section has invisible ink and the more sophisticated Enigma cipher machine. Interactive videos cover famous intelligence operations and more modern conflicts, such as the siege of London's Iranian embassy in 1980. Bringing the museum to life, Gallery Adventures are free kids' programs that run alongside special exhibitions. They include dramatic enactments of landmark moments, such as the great POW escapes from Colditz Castle. It all adds up to an amazing amount to see; one visit hardly seems enough.

EATS FOR KIDS Thankfully, the **café** is ration-free. It serves hot dogs, kids' meals, and other food for grown-ups. Those who bring their own lunch can eat in a picnic room on the lower ground floor or outside if the weather's fine. Good supplies can be found at sandwich shops in nearby Kennington Road.

KENSINGTON GARDENS

Of all the London parks, Kensington Gardens is essentially the children's park, with its Peter Pan connections, wide open spaces, boating lake, and the latest addition, the Princess Diana Memorial Playground. It was she who put Kensington on the map—and the world's newspapers—and was probably the most famous resident of Kensington Palace, situated on the edge of the park.

Although Kensington Gardens seems to merge into Hyde Park, the Long Water, which leads into the Serpentine boating lake, separates the two spaces. William III chose the fresh air and peaceful green fields of Kensington for his family home, and over 300 years later, the park still has that rambling, wild feel, far from the noise of busy Bayswater Road to the north and Kensington Gore to the south. There are tranquil, formal gardens with fountains and paths to run around in the elegant Italian Gardens, to the north of the Long Water, near Lancaster Gate. The long Flower Walk, at the opposite end of the park, is a joy, with endless displays to admire throughout the year. Along the Long Water, a bronze Peter Pan

EATS FOR KIDS The chalet-style **Park Café** (Princess Diana Memorial Playground) serves fun food to match the mood. Try a Serpentine and Elf sandwich (ham, cheese, bacon, chicken, and tomatoes) or Birdkeeper's Wings (chicken wings with cheese sauce). There are salads and fries, too. Outside the park, off Bayswater Road, the **Mandarin Kitchen** (14 Queensway, tel. 020/7727–9012) bustles with diners digging into barbecued pork and vegetables. Kids might want to share a bowl of fried rice or noodles. Kensington High Street has plentiful possibilities; for sandwiches and coffee, the slick **Pret a Manger** (Unit 14 Kensington Arcade, Kensington High St., tel. 020/7938–1110) is tops.

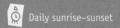

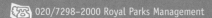

Bordered by Bayswater Rd., Long Water, Kensington Gore, Kensington Palace Gardens. Tube: High Street Kensington, Lancaster Gate, Queensway

 Free

 Daily sunrise–sunset

020/7298–2000 Royal Parks Management

All ages

statue is set in an enchanted woodland area, where kids can hide behind bushes. He plays his pipe to fairies and rabbits, which pop out almost magically from the gnarled, treelike base of the statue. To the west of this is the Round Pond, where children sail toy boats and swans glide; if you're here when daylight fades, you may see bats flitting over the water.

The Princess Diana Memorial Playground, near the Black Lion Gate park entrance and the Queensgate tube, explores the Peter Pan theme even further, with beautiful wood equipment amid the grass. Children can climb and swashbuckle away thanks to a pirate galleon, wigwams, and a magical fountain. Don't miss the old Elfin Oak by the playground. Sculpted in the bark of the slightly hollowed stump, fairies, elves, and woodland animals look as if they could be charmed to life after dusk, when the visitors have gone home.

KEEP IN MIND
You can see 18th-century state rooms at Kensington Palace (tel. 020/7937–9561), where some of the formal royal dress collection is on display. It's open Monday–Saturday 9:30–4, Sunday 11–5.

HEY, KIDS! The creator of Peter Pan, J. M. Barrie lived just a short walk away at 100 Bayswater Road. It was on his many walks through Kensington Gardens that he met the Llewellyn-Davies boys, who were the inspiration for the Darling family and their adventures in Never Land.

KENWOOD HOUSE

43

On the edge of Hampstead Heath, between two charming old London villages, Hampstead and Highgate, lies Kenwood House. The reasons to visit it are many: you can tour the magnificent mansion, along the way seeing some wonderful paintings by the old masters. You can stroll its landscaped woodland gardens, or you can mount the high covered viewing stand just outside the grounds for a great view of the green space that exists so close to the city.

As befits a mansion built by Robert Adam in 1764 for the Lord Chancellor, Lord Mansfield, the house has sumptuous rooms. Of them, the library is in a league of its own, with classic, templelike ceiling decor and columns that astound and amaze. Kids might prefer the paintings, however, including some of the world's most famous. *The Guitar Player,* by Vermeer; Rembrandt's self-portrait; and *The Man with a Cane,* by Frans Hals, are included in a children's activity leaflet, which explains the house's history and highlights and prompts kids to write and draw their findings. Kids might also like the charming portraits of children,

KEEP IN MIND To get information on the Music on a Summer Evening series (July–August), call Kenwood House. Tickets are also on sale at the on-site box office.

EATS FOR KIDS Kenwood's **Brew House** (note the Guinness connection), in the spacious white stable and coach house, sells a lot more than beer. In fact it's a family restaurant, which, on weekends and during school vacations, serves kids' favorites, such as macaroni and cheese, chicken, sausages, and salmon. A selection of pastries and cakes make a scrumptious dessert. Walking back to Hampstead, you'll find **Spaniards Inn** (Spaniards Rd., tel. 020/8731–6571), a historic tollgate pub with paneled interior, log fires, and hot dishes of the day. The notorious highwayman Dick Turpin, gentle painter Joshua Reynolds, and the poet Shelley all rested here.

Hampstead La., NW3. Tube: Hampstead Free 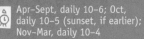 Apr–Sept, daily 10–6; Oct, daily 10–5 (sunset, if earlier); Nov–Mar, daily 10–4

020/8348–1286 All ages

including one of the Duke of Wellington's goddaughter; *Miss Murray,* by Lawrence; and Wright's exquisitely lit *Dressing the Kitten,* as well as some gorgeous Gainsborough society ladies. Tucked away upstairs is a curious collection of shoe buckles—the sparkly ones would make hot fashion today.

Kenwood's other great treasure, its gardens, lead down to a lake with ducks and other waterbirds. In summer, this is the scene of outdoor evening concerts, a few of which end in spectacular firework displays. If you time your visit to coincide with an afternoon pre-concert rehearsal, you can picnic or throw a Frisbee with musical accompaniment. In late spring, the rhododendrons and azaleas near the house are ablaze with color; this is a great place for chasing and playing hide-and-seek, as is the ivy tunnel. Another, almost-secret spot is the enclosed Kitchen Gardens; you can jump from step to step on the sundial while telling the time. Just don't be in a hurry to leave.

HEY, KIDS! Edward Guinness, the first Earl of Iveagh, bought Kenwood to house his paintings in 1924, and in 1927 bequeathed the collection to the nation. (In the poorer parts of London, he also set up houses for those who couldn't afford them.) The Guinness family wealth came from the now well-known brewing business. The beer that bears the family name is the tall black brew known as stout, which has its roots in Ireland, although it is now brewed worldwide.

KEW BRIDGE STEAM MUSEUM

Steam along to this fascinating little museum with big steam engines, housed in a former Victorian pumping station. Each weekend, a working collection of these terrific engines is cranked up by a team of enthusiasts, who also love to answer your questions and explain how these humongous pieces of machinery used to do the vital job of pumping water.

This particular pumping station supplied west London for over a century, and the steam hall once housed six boilers. Three-level walkways enable you to appreciate the beasts' full size, and the operating machines let you experience a slightly steamy atmosphere. Now imagine a time when all the boilers were fired up and a team of brawny men hand-shoveled coal. This is a good trip for any kid who likes to see how things work, but the brightly painted beams, pumps, pistons, and flywheels—living sculptures that sing, hiss, and sigh with steam—also appeal to kids who just like to look at cool stuff. The engines have romantic names and interesting stories. Dancers End Twin Beam used to pump water to Lord Rothschild's country estate. The Grand Junction 90-incher, one of the Cornish beam

EATS FOR KIDS Only open on weekends noon–2, the **Babcock Café,** in the old boiler room (Babcock was a Victorian engineer), serves lunchtime food that is far from old or boiled. You might find baked salmon, chicken curry, or vegetarian bakes, plus a soup of the day and sandwiches, on the daily changing menu. Main meals are from £4, and smaller kids' portions are available. On weekdays, bring a picnic, and eat in the steam hall or by the waterwheel outside if the weather is fine.

 Green Dragon La., Brentford.
Rail: Kew Bridge

 020/8568-4757;
www.cre.canon.co.uk/~davide/kbsm

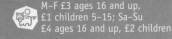 M–F £3 ages 16 and up,
£1 children 5–15; Sa–Su
£4 ages 16 and up, £2 children

 Daily 11–5

 8 and up

engines that originally pumped here, is the largest 20-ton working engine of its type in the world (in action 3–3:30 weekends). At full tilt it delivered 472 gallons per stroke. Another, larger Cornish engine (a 100-incher not back in working order yet) pumped 717 gallons per stroke.

The Water for Life gallery is a little more hands-on. It shows how the water system in London has worked since Roman times. You can even walk through a cross section of the modern Thames Water Ring Main. Ask for a kids' activity and information sheet, which brings some of the exhibits—but not the sewer rats—to life.

Kids who like steam locomotives (picture Thomas the Tank Engine) should visit the two beauties in the engine shed. Even better, come on a weekend when free short rides are offered, so kids can let off some steam of their own.

HEY, KIDS! Sewers, rats, and the slightly revolting world underneath London have a magnetic appeal. Can you actually imagine anything more horrible than people scratching around in them trying to make a living? These poor souls were called "toshers," which comes from the English slang for rubbish: tosh.

KEEP IN MIND In addition to regular railway weekends, there are a whole host of special event weekends, including a live model-railway show, a festival of steam, and a historic fire-engine rally. The Stand Pipe Tower opens occasionally for intrepid stair climbers.

LEGOLAND

41

Lego lovers and Duplo devotees have a ball at this attraction that combines fun and creativity in a series of play and discovery zones. Imagine those famous building bricks becoming larger than life and taking shape as all sorts of figures. Imagine going on over 50 rides or building to your heart's content. This Lego-theme park lets your family do just that, and it's constantly being updated and added to with the latest kid trends in mind.

In enchanting Miniland, Europe's most historic and exciting places come to life. Big Ben chimes, Tower Bridge opens to let boats through, Paris bustles with cars, and the Millennium Dome hopefully manages a better fate than the original. Soccer fans can see a match at Wembley Stadium, and an airport zone featuring a 90-foot-long jumbo jet is scheduled to lift off in 2001.

Dinosaurs, dragons, pirates, rats, and mythical beasts inhabit a selection of rides from low-level whizzing to high-level zooming. Rides are geared to a range of ages, so little

HEY, KIDS!
Can you guess how many bricks it takes to build the models here? More than you've got at home, for sure. The Dinosaur Family took a quarter million bricks, but maybe you could make a mini version of Little Egg, the smallest member of the family.

KEEP IN MIND Summer, particularly during school vacation, is the busiest time here, so if you come then, come early to avoid lines for the top rides. Summer is also the time when the most attractions are open. Check for special events, such as fireworks evenings, stunt shows, and other performances. As you'd expect, the shop sells Lego in vast quantities; any piece of Lego you ever wanted can be found here.

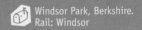 Windsor Park, Berkshire.
Rail: Windsor

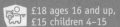 £18 ages 16 and up,
£15 children 4–15

 Mar–late July and early Sept–Jan,
daily 10–6 (sunset, if earlier);
late July–early Sept, daily 10–8

08705/040404;
www.legoland.co.uk

 All ages

ones don't miss out. In Duplo Gardens, kids can get wet or fly to tree-top height in the Whirly Bird helicopter. In the Lego Traffic zone, children test their skill at the boating or driving school (there's an easier version for smaller kids). Lego technicians can mess about in My Town's garage or discover the world's wonders, from jungle to polar regions, in the Explorer's Institute. Big screams emanate from the Wild Woods zone's Pirate Falls, where a camera captures you at splashdown. Another fast wet one not to miss is the Jet Ski Wave Surfer. Longer-distance rides, such as Riding the Dragon and the Ferris wheel, yield good views of the park. The list of instant entertainment options is endless, and that's not including the Creation Centre, where you can pick up tips from the pros who make the models.

Parents love the clean, attractive environment, with immaculate gardens and tranquil resting spots. Thanks to its special hands-on approach, Legoland is a winner hands down.

EATS FOR KIDS In true Lego fashion, **Pizza Pergola, Pasta Patch,** and the **Harbourside** restaurants let you roll up to your favorite flavor (be it pizza, pasta, or stir-fry), choose your own fresh ingredients, and watch your perfect lunch take shape before your eyes. For burgers from the grill, fight your way to the **Crossed Ribs,** near Pirate Falls in the Wild Woods zone.

LONDON AQUARIUM

A cross the water from Big Ben, deep beneath County Hall lurks a microcosm of underwater life. Here dappled, curving corridors are lined with glass tanks containing an amazing variety of fish and other water creatures. Displays of sea and river settings are divided into sections representing the waters of the world. Spend too long in the early sections, and your eyes will bulge out—just like the fish. A good exploration takes about two hours, allowing time to hear a talk by a marine expert, feel around in the tide pools, and linger in areas that you'd otherwise have to rush through, such as the mangrove swamps toward the end.

Your journey begins with the birdsong, grass reeds, and creatures that inhabit the freshwater of Britain and Europe. Adults may want to stay in this gentle re-creation a little longer than kids, who, after being momentarily fascinated by the luminous moon jellyfish, switch their attention to the Pacific's sharks. Swishing around between schools of smaller fish fry (the jacks), they bare their fiendish flesh-tearing teeth and flash a perpetually

EATS FOR KIDS The aquarium has no restaurant, but you can eat a picnic in a seating area with drink machines. (Waterloo station has many sandwich stands.) For fishy dishes with chips, dive into the reasonably priced cab driver's haunt **Super Fish** (191 Waterloo Rd., tel. 020/7928–6924). Also see BFI London IMAX Cinema and HMS *Belfast*.

County Hall, Westminster Bridge Rd., SE1.
Tube: Waterloo, Westminster

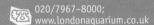 £8.50 ages 15 and up,
£6.50 students,
£5 children 3–14

 Daily 10–6

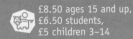 020/7967–8000;
www.londonaquarium.co.uk

 3 and up

hungry look from their beady eyes. Circle the super-size cylindrical tank again and again as it sinks down three floors to where the wonderful rays hunker down beneath the sand. At each level you can sit and stare through the almost floor-height glass, so even tiny tots get a great look. At intervals, TV monitors show fishy documentaries, and interactive audiovisual displays let kids press buttons to find out how, for instance, the smallest fish survive.

Another don't-miss section is Seashore and Beach, where you can stroke a ray and watch such tide-pool creatures as crabs and anemones. If kids can drag themselves away from hand-dipping, they can check out the moving, darting rainbow of color of the Coral Reef, with gorgeously painted clown fish, the impressive lionfish with its venomous spines, delicate sea horses, and teeny spotted garden eels popping up from the sand. Entertaining tricks they don't do, but these guys will have you hooked for hours nonetheless.

HEY, KIDS! Ever wonder if sharks sleep? The answer is very few do and rarely, since they must swim to keep water moving over their gills. However, the nurse shark does nap on the seabed. Want something else to chew on? A sand tiger shark can go through 20,000 teeth in a lifetime. Bet that bankrupts the tooth fairy!

KEEP IN MIND As you enter, note the feeding and aquatic talk times. Generally, shark and rain-forest talks are held daily; sharks are fed Tuesday, Thursday, and Saturday at 2:30; and piranhas chow down on Monday, Wednesday, Friday, and Saturday at 1, but times can change. Kids' activity and information sheets are 15p–30p, and a safari booklet (£3) gives valuable information that will last long after the visit.

LONDON BUTTERFLY HOUSE

A tiny piece of rain forest survives at the parking lot of Syon Park, west London (on the opposite riverbank from the Royal Botanic Gardens at Kew). It's a butterfly house—an exotic little oasis (mainly under glass roofs and with controlled humidity) where around 1,000 little beauties and some interesting creepy crawlies live among tropical plants that grow in a garden beside a gentle cascade and pool.

The delicate little beasts are everywhere: fluttering around your head, on the plants, and even on the paths, so step carefully. Feast your eyes on *Delias eucharis, Attacus atlas,* and *Danaus plexippus*—some of the brightest of the over 75 tropical species here. You can pick out your favorites from the signs by the door. Some butterflies are attracted by the color or scent of your clothes, so you may find them alighting on your back and shoulders. While you wander and admire them, the butterflies are busy getting on with their life cycle by feeding, mating, and dying (the odd corpse does lie around). You can read all about them by the little netted boxes, where you see pupae hanging on little lines.

HEY, KIDS!

Butterfly or moth? To tell the difference, look at the antennae. Butterflies have long, clublike antennae, whereas moths' are furry and featherlike. For a beautiful example, watch for the Giant Atlas moth, and compare it to the darting orange-and-black monarch butterfly.

KEEP IN MIND Just a few steps away from the butterfly house is another interesting animal attraction: the Aquatic Experience (*see above*). Another option, and one that's a welcome break after the butterfly house's humid conditions, is Syon Park (*see below*). No ordinary park, this sumptuous acreage contains the gardens that belonged to Syon House, home to the Duke of Northumberland. (There are separate admission charges for both attractions.) If you want to cram in everything, allow at least an hour for the butterflies, another for the aquatic animals, and as long as you can for the park—it's a beauty.

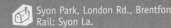 Syon Park, London Rd., Brentford.
Rail: Syon La.

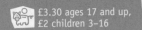 £3.30 ages 17 and up,
£2 children 3–16

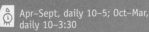 Apr–Sept, daily 10–5; Oct–Mar,
daily 10–3:30

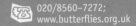 020/8560-7272;
www.butterflies.org.uk

 3 and up

The atmosphere is a little steamy, but it rapidly cools down when you pass into the neighboring British section, a semi-outdoor building. Look out for the large Purple Emperor, which thrives on a diet of deer droppings. Sharpen your eyesight to spot butterflies hiding underneath foliage or on the walls, as these Brit and European varieties are more timid than their tropical cousins.

The environment becomes humid again as you pass into the final section, the insect exhibit. Among the small selection of dangerous show insects, such as tarantulas and scorpions, you can see stick insects (or can you?), those wizards of camouflage. Don't miss the leopard geckos in the insect exhibit. Yes, they're lizards, but they're a lot cuter than the bugs and are a welcome addition.

EATS FOR KIDS The sweeping driveway into Syon Park is quite a hike, so you'll want to stay on the grounds to eat. Luckily, there are enough options here to satisfy. The self-service **Patio Café,** at the park entrance, serves pasta, sausages, chicken, snacks, and drinks. On the other side of the parking lot, the **Syon Park Farm Shop** sells enough delicious organic produce and snacks to make your own gourmet picnic.

LONDON DUNGEON

Blood, bones, and gore galore—what could be more appealing? The London Dungeon is the ultimate chamber of horrors, chronicling chilling periods in British history. You might think that children will find it too nightmarish—and some small ones do—yet strangely enough, there are hordes of children eager to be scared out of their wits, making for long lines to get in, particularly on weekends and during the holiday season.

The opening exhibit gives a taste of what's to come. Scarily lifelike wax models show how grim it could be to live in medieval times (around the 14th century). You'll find out what would happen if you stole a piece of bread to feed your starving kids (you could be hung) or spoke against the king (you could lose your tongue with the help of one of the torture instruments displayed here). If you didn't rot in prison with the rats, you might catch the plague, a pretty revolting fate, as demonstrated by a poor victim showing signs of the dreadful disease.

EATS FOR KIDS Drinks and the usual burger and fries fare is available from the on-site **restaurant.** Opposite, in Hays Galleria, **Café Rouge** (tel. 020/7378–0097) is a brasserie serving a range of club sandwiches, salads, and upscale chicken and burger dishes. Even cheaper is the historic **George Inn** (77 Borough High St., tel. 020/7407–2056), a five-minute walk away. Owned by the National Trust, it serves more traditional British fare.

 28–34 Tooley St., SE1. Tube:
London Bridge

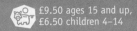 £9.50 ages 15 and up,
£6.50 children 4–14

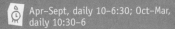 Apr–Sept, daily 10–6:30; Oct–Mar,
daily 10:30–6

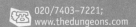 020/7403-7221;
www.thedungeons.com

 9 and up

But this is only the mild beginning of your tour, on which costumed actor-guides take you from one historical drama to another without warning. In Judgement Day, the first "ride," you may feel like an innocent bystander, but whether or not you're guilty of any crimes, somehow you know you won't escape courtroom punishment. Further journeys into the past are linked by dark catacomb-like passages lined with gruesome exhibits. In Jack the Ripper's London, for example, you'll witness tales of his terrible murders, after which he left his victims' insides out. In the final ride, try to survive the Great Fire of London in 1666 by running the gauntlet of flames—well, not actually, but the pyrotechnics are pretty convincing. If you do survive, you can take home a gory souvenir from the gift shop—severed arm, anyone?

The dungeon is billed as an orgy of grisly entertainment. Any child who relishes a churning stomach will think it's the best game in town.

KEEP IN MIND

Some of the exhibits, rides, and other parts of the tour are not advisable for people with weak hearts or nervous dispositions, pregnant women, or young children. Unaccompanied children under 15 are not admitted. You have been warned!

HEY, KIDS! London suffered from the Black Death, or bubonic plague, intermittently over 300 years. The first outbreak occurred in 1348. In 1665, the year of another major outbreak, Samuel Pepys recorded in his diary that 6,000 Londoners died in just one month. The disease, spread by flea-ridden rats, started with a rash, then fever, and swellings that turned black. Death would usually follow in two days.

LONDON PLANETARIUM

Climb aboard for an intergalactic space trip through the galaxies and a virtual tour into the future. This amazing, fast-moving, high-tech (Digistar) light show is a must for all space cadets and guaranteed to thrill even the less starry-eyed.

Before climbing the mock-rocket-lined stairs to the auditorium for your ride, however, you'll enter the Planet Zone. This atmospherically lit exhibit area—its walls lined with huge multicolor, textured planet models and changing video displays—is home to plentiful games, button pushing, and fun facts. Gravity is a big theme here. Step on the scales to compare your weight on Earth to that on Jupiter (with much more gravity); you'll be astounded at how big you've become. If you ate too many hot dogs out on the street, read your more comforting low-gravity Moon weight. Learn about ultimate gravity—a black hole—by spinning a ball around the perimeter of a black cone. Inevitably, it is sucked in by the powerful pull. On your way into the show, you can also find out how whispers, taps, and shouts travel from one end of the room to the other in sound waves.

HEY, KIDS!
Better watch out! Our galaxy is set on a collision course with neighbor Andromeda. But there's no need to brace for it this millennium, or even the next few. It will take at least another 5 billion years for the galaxies to collide.

EATS FOR KIDS **Pizza Express** (Baker St. and Marylebone Rd., tel. 020/ 7486–0888) is consistently good, with friendly staff in bright Italianate surroundings—although the pizzas aren't the biggest. Other possibilities on Baker Street include **Aroma** (118 Baker St., tel. 020/7224–3991), for delicious sandwiches and coffee, and **Reuben's** (79 Baker St., tel. 020/7486–0035), for gefilte fish, followed by a steak or salt-beef platter and other Jewish fare. Reuben's has upscale style (with prices to match) and a mittel-European deco-echo setting. See also Madame Tussaud's.

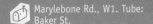
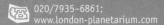
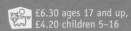
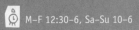

The show itself starts on Mars, 500 years from now. From there you take a high-speed "Hyper-Drive" star trek with lots of swooping and diving to loud zippy music. You almost want to hang onto your seat. Older kids might find the commentary a little tacky ("This is your captain speaking."), but the scenery is terrific and the facts are accessible and absorbing. Your astro-vocab will probably increase twofold. You'll surf by the sun, pull back from the heat, and zap off into the Milky Way and beyond, catching new stars and planet systems in the making and breaking (a supernova). You'll also teeter on the edge of one of those powerful, mysterious black holes, but don't worry. You'll be brought safely back to Mars and our own millennium.

KEEP IN MIND The planetarium is operated in conjunction with adjacent Madame Tussaud's (*see below*), and combination tickets are available (£13.45 ages 17 and up, £9 children 5-16). Don't just whisk through the planetarium after a visit to the waxworks, however. Allow two hours for a fun, fact-filled visit. Planetarium shows last about 20 minutes and run at frequent intervals throughout the day until 5, the last screening.

LONDON TRANSPORT MUSEUM

The best way to get around London hassle-free is by Underground—aka the tube. But have you ever wondered how it was built, particularly the parts that run under the Thames? Here's the place to find out. The story of London transportation is told with costumed actors, from the first tunnel in the 1860s (for steam engines on the Metropolitan Line from Paddington) to the 1990s' Canary Wharf station, designed by Norman Foster. The museum uses one of the original high steel-and-glass-ceiling Covent Garden flower market buildings, which gives an air of an old Victorian station.

Travel around the museum through numbered Kidzones. There's lots to pull, turn, spin, and feel while you uncover theories of horsepower or the best way to design a bus. Work sheets take kids on self-guiding trails and ask them to answer a series of questions, after which they get a stamp or cutout before passing to the next zone. The Numeracy trail gets children searching for statistics—counting passengers and tube stops, checking out bus routes and license plates. Younger kids stay amused with the Thomas the Tank trail, which

HEY, KIDS! If you were a young kid hanging around town in the 1880s, you could have earned a penny or two by sweeping horse dung off the streets. In those days, the most streamlined city transportation was the horse tram, and London's horse-drawn trams produced 1,000 tons of dung a day—a nice little moneymaker for eager kids!

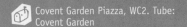

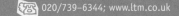
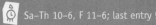

includes all the colorful characters and engines from the popular stories.

In addition to the trails, there are costumed actor-guides, who love to talk about their jobs, from sweepers in front of the first horse-drawn steam buses to firemen on steam trains to wartime bus conductors. There are also audiovisual sections to explore. In the oral history archive, you can listen to true-life experiences of people who kept the capital moving during World War II, which was pretty harrowing. In the film archive, wonderful black-and-white footage shows how the Metropolitan Railway took shape from 1905. You can also get a taste of what it looks like to drive a tube train down a curvy dark tunnel—not a job for the timid.

The last stop is usually the gift shop, full of sensibly priced souvenirs like an old tram or a little red double-decker bus.

KEEP IN MIND Summer vacation brings even more activities. You may be able to join in a craft workshop, look at special small model displays, or take a seat on board some of the real vehicles, which are not usually open to the public.

EATS FOR KIDS The museum has a space to eat any goodies you buy from one of the numerous sandwich shops that line the piazza and surrounding streets. For a cheap vegetarian lunch, the stalwart **Food for Thought** (31 Neal St., tel. 020/7836–0239) is a short walk away, north of the tube. A bright and buzzy basement with squashed-together tables, it offers daily specials as well as soup, mega-salads, and yummy desserts, all on the healthful side. Also see Covent Garden and the Theatre Museum.

LONDON ZOO

Once upon a visit, the London Zoo displayed its animals boringly, cage after cage. It took the threat of closure some years ago to punch things up, and today the zoo is exciting. Activities go far beyond watching and meeting the 12,000 animals housed here, and it's unlikely you'll cover everything. So come early and allow yourself several hours.

Naturally, the big beasts are a must-see. Sometimes it's difficult to get a good look, however, since some of the larger enclosures have obscuring foliage and private areas to let the endangered species take part in the captive breeding programs. The family of the magnificent Sumatran tiger Raika is one of these success stories. At the rejuvenated Bear Mountain, rare sloth bears live alongside lively langurs; you can find out how harmoniously these neighbors coexist at the afternoon bear talk.

For a chance to pet an animal, head to the Amphitheatre, where encounter sessions could include leaping lemurs or flying parrots. Some areas have keepers on hand to

HEY, KIDS!

They may be the planet's smallest inhabitants, but in population, invertebrates dwarf humans. Next time you swat a fly, just think: if a pair of houseflies and a year's worth of descendants survived, they would form a ball 93 million miles across—the distance from Earth to the sun.

EATS FOR KIDS Since you're a captive audience, prices are a little higher at the **Fountain Café** than outside the zoo, but the portions are good size. The menu contains a large selection of hot and cold meals and snacks. The **Picnic Shop** is a cheaper option, selling self-serve, packaged snacks to eat at the outdoor tables. Better still, put together your own meal from **Marks & Spencer** (143 Camden High St., tel. 020/ 7267–6055), a grocery store close to the Camden Town Underground station. There are many grassy areas in which to sit.

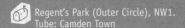 Regent's Park (Outer Circle), NW1.
Tube: Camden Town

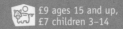 £9 ages 15 and up,
£7 children 3–14

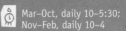 Mar–Oct, daily 10–5:30;
Nov–Feb, daily 10–4

 020/7722–3333;
www.londonzoo.co.uk

 2 and up

answer questions both in and outside the specified public feeding times. At the elephant house, you can meet Dilberta, once an abandoned baby and now the biggest elephant here, as you can witness at her daily weigh-in. You can pet more common but no-less-engaging animals, from tiny rabbits to sheep, horses, and camels, at the Children's Zoo. Younger kids love to ride horse or llama carriages at Riding Square.

The most important beasts on the planet, however, are insects, and you can find out why in the Web of Life. Combining an art workshop and play area, this great new section gets kids to explore the fine balance between humans and other animals. Watching the teeny leaf-cutter ants at work, marching along a rope, is as enthralling as watching the fiercest mammals. Children may also touch various minibeasts, such as giant millipedes and scorpions, and question the keepers. If you have time (a big IF), visit the breeding section upstairs, which has a good selection of tropical patula snails.

KEEP IN MIND Consider these two ways to plan your day. You can follow the green footprint trail, which follows a circular route past the major exhibits; it can take all day in and of itself. Or you can shuttle between feeding times and animal-encounter sessions, noted on the Daily Events Sheet (available at the entrance). You may want to strike a balance between the two, as fatigue dictates.

MADAME TUSSAUD'S

This world-famous museum brimming with wax models of famous and infamous individuals hardly needs an introduction. Its popularity is evidenced by the continual lines of tourist buses outside. But the life of Madame herself is less known than her celebrated handiwork. The young Tussaud learned her skills from a doctor, who introduced her to French society, including time spent at the court of Versailles. During the French Revolution, young Marie was captured (because of her royal association), but though she turned a few heads, she never lost her own. She did, however, make countless death masks of nobles executed on the guillotine. Ever the hardheaded businesswoman, she took these gruesome models to England as the nucleus of a touring exhibition and never returned to France. The exhibit has been here since 1884.

You follow a set route that includes the 200 Years section, containing some of the original revolutionary heads and revealing how models are made. In the Garden Party, you can mingle with the rich and famous: Mel Gibson, Brad Pitt, Arnold Schwarzenegger, among other stars.

KEEP IN MIND Assuming you have the time, it's well worth visiting the London Planetarium (*see above*), next door. That way, you can experience both earthly and inter-galactic stargazing. A discounted combination ticket costs £13.95 for ages 17 and up, £9.50 for children 5–16. The information number above takes credit-card bookings for timed tickets, so you can avoid standing in line, but there is an added £1 charge.

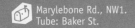 Marylebone Rd., NW1.
Tube: Baker St.

 0870/400-3000;
www.madame-tussauds.com

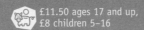 £11.50 ages 17 and up,
£8 children 5–16

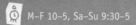 M–F 10–5, Sa–Su 9:30–5

 7 and up

Kids might not know them all (a pricey color guide lists everyone), but watch for that English children's book rascal Just William, who spies on a bunch of cricketers from behind a wall.

You pass into the Sporting Heroes hall, including some of the latest Olympians and tennis champions, and then on to Hollywood Legends and Superstars, followed by historical superstars, such as Abe Lincoln, Tony Blair, Nelson Mandela, and good old Will Shakespeare. It's all a tame precursor to the big thrill, however. In the Chamber of Horrors, tortured victims and infamous killers populate a world of scary sounds, scenery, and smells. Younger kids might not have the stomach for it, and an escape route is available. The Spirit of London takes you on a black cab ride through centuries of London history, from the medieval plague to the swinging 1960s. No doubt Tussaud is smiling, not turning, in her grave.

HEY, KIDS! Real human hair is used on the models and requires regular grooming. It isn't supposed to need a cut! But staff were spooked to discover that Adolf Hitler's appeared to be growing.

EATS FOR KIDS Madame Tussaud's has a **restaurant,** located just after the Chamber of Horrors. If your kids still have an appetite, they can sample the usual kiddie range of pizza slices, fries, burgers, and breaded chicken nuggets. Also see London Planetarium.

Not just any bridge, this over-1,200-foot aluminum-and-steel span is the first new bridge in central London in over a century. (The Romans built the first pedestrian bridge across the Thames, and the last was Tower Bridge in 1894.) What's even more impressive, however, is that it's car-free. While traffic buzzes across Blackfriars to the west and London Bridge to the east, pedestrians wander across in peace, stopping to admire the beautiful views. As modern as it is, the bridge connects the old (elegant domed St. Paul's Cathedral) and the new (stark, red, oversize Tate Modern) and stands smack in the middle of the Millennium Mile, a new South Bank walk that takes in a clutch of popular sights.

The bridge opened in a blaze of publicity on a breezy weekend in June 2000, and people lined up by the thousands to enjoy the so-called "blaze of light" streaking across the Thames. It does appear to fly over the water with effortless grace, but the very fact

EATS FOR KIDS Buy gourmet sandwiches from **Sarnis** (Gabriel's Wharf, tel. 020/7928–6654) and picnic in Bernie Spain Gardens, beside the OXO Tower. Or choose from 40 types of sweet and savory pancakes at **House of Crêpes** (Gabriel's Wharf, tel. 020/7401–9816). Also see St. Paul's Cathedral and Tate Modern.

KEEP IN MIND After walking the bridge, why not walk the Millennium Mile? Actually, this much-visited section of river contains two other walks: the Thames Path National Trail and the Jubilee Walk (marked by 1977 Silver Jubilee discs soon to be replaced by discs for the Gold Jubilee in 2002). On your way, pop in to the free, lively, Museum of _____ (The Bargehouse, OXO Tower Wharf, Bargehouse St., tel. 020/7401–2255), so named because the museum's theme changes every few months. Since its inception, it has metamorphosed into the Museum of Emotions, Museum of Me, and Museum of the Unknown.

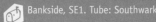 Bankside, SE1. Tube: Southwark

 Free

 Daily 24 hrs

020/7403–8299 Southwark
Information Centre, London Bridge

 All ages

of its lightness, plus the overwhelming hordes on that first weekend, sent the state-of-the-art bridge swaying. Visitors had their moving experience all right, but even though some swinging is expected with suspension bridges, the engineers were unsettled enough to close it.

Subject to completion of further stabilization, you can again put the bridge at the top of your itinerary, if for no other reason than that it's a joy to cross the water without cars thundering beside you. The views are breathtaking, none more so than St. Paul's in all its glory looming before you—the best river view of the cathedral and an artistic photo op. You can look downriver to the Tower of London, Tower Bridge, and beyond, and up to Somerset House, with the London Eye and Big Ben rising above the river bend. Down below, boats bustle back and forth. Don't forget to give a wave to people on the sightseeing boats, who don't have the same chance you do to stop and enjoy.

HEY, KIDS! Christopher Wren, the architect of St. Paul's, might have given up if he'd had the same problems the builders of this bridge had. Work that was already behind schedule came to a sudden halt so that a rare breed of snail found on some old jetty legs could be rehoused, to the tune of more than £50,000. It just goes to show that small creatures can wield big power.

MONUMENT

The simply named monument designed by Christopher Wren to commemorate the Great Fire of London and its victims in 1666 was the tallest single column in the world when it was completed in 1677. Scaling its 311 steps is not for the fainthearted or weary and is guaranteed to tire even the most hyper kid. At 202 feet, the summit is the same distance from the base as the site where the fire began, at a bakery in Pudding Lane. A trip to the top rewards climbers with a wonderful view of Wren's London and today's.

The story of the Great Fire is a cruel one. It raged for days, turning the city into an inferno. When it finally burned itself out, 87 churches and 13,200 houses had been lost and all that remained were the smoking ruins of the medieval walled city. The only blessing was that it solved London's overcrowding problem in one blow.

While the city's destruction is represented by a gilt bronze urn licked by flames on top of the Monument, inscriptions around the base chart King Charles II's efforts to rebuild London

KEEP IN MIND A joint ticket is available for the Monument and Tower Bridge Experience. Climbing the Monument is not recommended for those with claustrophobia or carrying babies or for small children. Indeed it shudders with the passing of each vehicle below. The famous diarist James Boswell found the experience unnerving: ". . . so monstrous a way up in the air, so far above London and all its spires." An earlier diarist, Samuel Pepys, wrote commentary that's now used in a small video reenactment illuminating the Great Fire in the Museum of London (*see below*).

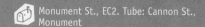

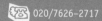 Monument St., EC2. Tube: Cannon St., Monument

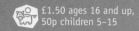 £1.50 ages 16 and up, 50p children 5–15

 Daily 10–6

 020/7626–2717

7 and up

with the help of Christopher Wren. The view from the top testifies to the latter's genius. You may be able to locate some of his most famous churches nearby, such as St. Stephen Walbrook, St. Bride's, and St. Mary-le-Bow, although his work doesn't predominate as remarkably as it did 300 years ago, when St. Paul's was the tallest building in the skyline. Now the cathedral is dwarfed by the tall techno towers of the City, such as the Nat West Tower and the Lloyd's building. Back then it was a once-in-a-lifetime, jelly-leg experience to mount the steps and walk out onto the viewing platform—and, horribly, also a popular suicide spot, until a safety cage was built.

For your efforts, you will be rewarded with a special certificate to prove that you made it to the top.

HEY, KIDS! When the old St. Paul's Cathedral began to burn during the height of the fire, molten lead from its roof rained down onto the streets. Wren, the architect of the Monument, was soon put to work after the fire to build a bigger, greater St. Paul's.

EATS FOR KIDS Weekdays, when the City is in full buzz, visit **Fuego** (1A Pudding La., tel. 020/7929–3366), a Spanish restaurant aptly named after the Great Fire. The many tapas (small dishes) and larger menu choices, such as battered prawns, a steak sandwich with fries and salad, and paella, can be shared. On the weekend, when City places are closed, cross London Bridge to the bistro-style **Café Rouge** (Hays Galleria, off Tooley St., tel. 020/7378–0097), which has more steak and fries, chicken, and steak sandwiches.

MOUNTFITCHET CASTLE

Castles and kids just go together, and this castle in the Essex countryside is a prime destination. It's a Norman "motte and bailey" (a walled feudal castle atop a hill), with dwellings reconstructed from ruins. To visit is to imagine life for common peasants and Norman lords and ladies 900 years ago.

Don't be charmed by the folksy huts and buildings. After a look inside, you realize life was anything but charming, though the deer, hens, and goats that wander around *are* cute. (The castle shop sells food packets to feed them.) Otherwise, life was tough, as you'll learn while walking around the signposted huts, where waxwork models—blacksmith, brewer, weaver, alchemist, potter, cook, candlemaker—go about and tell about (with voice recordings) their daily toils.

Grim reminders of the punishment on offer are apparent. In the prison you see a victim with his hand freshly chopped off—he'd probably stolen some of the castle's deer. The

KEEP IN MIND As the village and parkland is outside, plan to visit in good weather. Should the day dampen, head to the House on the Hill Toy Museum, next door (10% off admission with castle ticket). It holds a fair-size collection, from teddy bears to Victorian trains.

EATS FOR KIDS A **café** here serves a small range of food from this century, and if the weather's good, you can picnic on the pretty grounds. Stansted village has tea shops and village pubs for hot meals, but in the nearby village of Rickling Green (heading north, just off B1383), the **Cricketers Arms** (Rickling Village Green, tel. 01799/543210) is recommended. At this pub, you can order sandwiches, steaks, and children's meals among cozy cricketing memorabilia.

Stansted, Essex.
Rail: Stansted, Mountfitchet

01279/813237;
www.gold.enta.net

£4.50 ages 15 and up,
£3.50 children 3–14

Mid-Mar–mid-Nov, daily 10–5

4 and up

offender hanging from the gallows would have committed a more serious crime, while the stocks, which you can try on for size, were for petty misdemeanors. You wouldn't dare get sick either; take a look inside the surgeon's hut, which more closely resembles a butcher's room. If you want to know more about anything you see, ask one of the costumed villagers strolling around. You may even meet the baron Richard de Montfitchet or his lady.

The castle walls kept out invaders, so to live inside them was a privilege—hard to believe when you peek in the community house where 30 people would have lived with their animals. Climb up the siege tower to look for rebels, and find out how to stop them with the dastardly looking, towering catapult, which took 15 men to operate. Defense wasn't always successful; in the peasant's hut, you learn of a ransack by the feared Vikings. It's a wild, wild world to discover, and you'll be jolly thankful you can return to the comfort of modern times.

HEY, KIDS! The grassy surroundings here are a far cry from the nasty conditions you would have seen in Norman times. Back then, it would have been muddy and full of foul smells, rats, and disease. Even the baron would have to endure beggars and dogs eating scraps off the floor in the banqueting hall, thrown by the generous diners.

MUSEUM OF LONDON

Anything you ever wanted to know about London is here, in the world's largest urban-history museum. From prehistoric times to the present, you can explore more than a million exhibits, arranged by historical period, and get added information from computers placed nearby. The best way to navigate is to follow the "catwalk" (the cat features in the tale of the legendary Lord Mayor of London, Dick Whittington), which takes you chronologically. It starts with early cavemen and continues through Londinium (Roman London), when the city became known in the civilized world. Along the way, you can touch and explore, discovering, for instance, how everyday tools like weighing machines worked. Rooms usually contain costumed guides, such as the young Roman servant girl who tells about her life and her wealthy employers and answers questions. Along the Victorian street, you can peer into the windows of the mock shops, particularly the confectioner's, with its huge jars of traditional sticky sweets. A costumed shopkeeper might tell you about the wares on sale and even give you a sample. It's a good idea on arrival to check about availability.

EATS FOR KIDS The **café** does a good job at soups, salads, sandwiches, and cakes. **Coffee Republic** (47 London Wall, tel. 020/7588–2220) also has good sandwiches along with better coffee, but remember that this place, as with most everything in the city's financial district, shuts down on weekends. Your best bet then is the **Crypt Café** (St. Paul's Churchyard, tel. 020/7236–4128), beneath the arches at St. Paul's Cathedral. For children, there's mozzarella pizza or chicken nuggets, with ice cream and drink (£4.25); for adults, there are gourmet main salads and fish or meat dishes, all in the company of illustrious tombs.

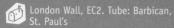

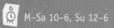
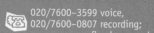

You should also find out if a Touch and Feel session is scheduled. In these wonderful programs, you get to handle objects that have been dug up from beneath the streets or the riverbed by the museum's busy archaeological department. Just imagine feeling the smooth worn leather on an ancient sandal that might have once tramped about these very streets.

Modern London is represented by such wacky fashions as the shoes created by Vivienne Westwood, which were so high even supermodels toppled off them. You can spot an eye-catching carnival float from the famous Notting Hill Carnival summer festival and the traditional glitzy coach still used by the Lord Mayor for his annual parade. And don't forget to look out for the remains of the original Londinium Roman wall, in the courtyard, the source of the museum street's name—London Wall.

KEEP IN MIND

Tickets are good for one year, for both the permanent gallery and the temporary exhibitions. It's one of the best ticket deals in town.

HEY, KIDS! As the story goes, Dick Whittington came to London to seek his fortune, but when he didn't make any money, he turned tail. As he was leaving, he looked back on the city, and the church bells, along with a black cat, told him to "turn again, Whittington." He did, and he became a great mayor four times over between 1391 and 1419.

NATIONAL ARMY MUSEUM

More compact than the Imperial War Museum, this army museum tells the soldier's story—from Henry V's campaign against the French in 1415, when the English archers won at Agincourt (which the Brits have never let their neighbors forget), to today's less-deadly trade clashes with France. Other chronicled campaigns include Wellington versus Napoleon (don't miss the skeleton of the general's favorite horse and the saw used for rapid on-field amputations—ouch!) and the English redcoats versus the American patriots in the American Revolution.

Wonderful battlefield models show the strategies employed, while life-size uniformed models are faithfully reproduced. Looking at them close up is interesting enough, but you can even try some pieces on, such as a heavy, uncomfortable helmet from the English Civil War. (In that war, the Republican Roundheads, led by Oliver Cromwell, fought the more dashingly dressed Royalist Cavaliers to defeat the monarchy.) In a display of arms and armor, you can test a cannonball's weight; imagine if it landed close by in battle.

KEEP IN MIND The souvenir shop here is a great place for fanatics of all things war, both national and international. You'll find model soldiers and a good range of books on the subject.

EATS FOR KIDS The museum's **café** offers light meals, but for a budget main dish, such as spaghetti Bolognese, for around £5, and a dessert of the day, the **Stockpot** (273 King's Rd., tel. 020/7823–3175) and neighbor **Chelsea Kitchen** (98 King's Rd., tel. 020/7589–1330) are hard to beat.

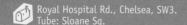 Royal Hospital Rd., Chelsea, SW3.
Tube: Sloane Sq.

 Free

 Daily 10–5:30

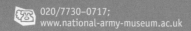 020/7730-0717;
www.national-army-museum.ac.uk

 6 and up

The modern army is covered through re-creations of a World War I trench and a Burmese jungle, as well as archival footage from both world wars, a piece of the Berlin Wall, and exhibits on the Gulf War and the Balkans. An interactive computer section tests your military skills, from recognizing uniforms and insignia of various regiments to surviving in a jungle expeditionary force.

During summer vacation, aspects of the museum come to life. A costumed guide may play an archer from the Middle Ages or a female dispatch rider from World War II. An actor might demonstrate one of the many important jobs behind the front line; during the Crimean War, for instance, Florence Nightingale's team of nurses made their mark. The museum is by the grassy grounds of the Royal Hospital, built by Wren as a retirement home for old or wounded soldiers. Look out for Chelsea Pensioners, resident veterans in red military-style coats and tricorn hats, unchanged since Wren's time.

HEY, KIDS! In the 18th century, women weren't allowed in the army, but some disguised themselves as soldiers and went anyway. Some went purely for the adventure; others were trying to find husbands or boyfriends who were missing.

NATIONAL GALLERY

More than 2,000 pictures by western Europe's great masters are displayed in this vast collection. What's more, you can see them for free. The pillared building is an integral part of one of London's most famous landmarks, Trafalgar Square, with its fountains, lions, Nelson's Column, and those pesky pigeons that will do anything for a crumb—even pose in your photos. The museum is a great place to see world-famous paintings or to spend an hour or two dodging the rain.

With such a vast wealth at your disposal, where to start? You could pick a period, such as the Renaissance, and go see the real Madonna, *The Virgin of the Rocks,* by Leonardo da Vinci, hung in the modern Sainsbury Wing. The West Wing has Titian and Holbein, the painter who made it big by painting such kings as Henry VIII. Then skip a century or two to the North Wing, for Dutch masters like Vermeer and Rembrandt, and move on to the East Wing for the Venice of Canaletto, the very British Constable, sea battles and sunsets by Turner, the France of Monet, and other celebrated Impressionists—van Gogh

KEEP IN MIND Have a pencil ready for filling out the tour booklets, because the museum is one place that does not supply you with one. There are some great pencils to choose from in the gallery's shops at the side entrance on Orange Street, however. They also have beautiful posters, drawing pads, and postcards. The Orange Street Shop at the Education Centre is open weekdays.

Trafalgar Sq., WC2. Tube: Charing Cross

 Free

 W 10–8:30, Th–T 10–6

 020/7747–2885;
www.national gallery.org.uk

 7 and up

and Cézanne. You can fine-tune your visit on-line in the Micro Gallery, where you can print out added information along with a personally planned tour—great for older kids.

Self-guiding themed tour booklets, good for children 7–11, direct you to different parts of the gallery and invite kids to look, think, draw, or write poems. They're really fun. One recent example was a bug-busting booklet stuffed with quirky facts and jokes; you'd never guess the gallery had so many paintings crawling with insects. On Saturday mornings at 11:30 and during summer vacation, there are often special talks and workshops for kids, which follow one artist or one piece of work. By exploring with your children, you'll end up seeing more than you expected. Or take advantage of their being diverted and sneak around the rest of the room in peace. You'll all feel more culturally enriched for the experience.

HEY, KIDS! Did you know that crushed-up insects make the beautiful red paint called carmine? Old masters used the red pigment from dead female kermes beetles, and a similar dye, known as cochineal (from the insect of the same name), was also used.

EATS FOR KIDS The self-service café, **Pret a Manger,** in the basement of the main building, is open daily until 5:30 (8:30 Wednesdays) for sandwiches, snacks, and drinks. **Texas Embassy Cantina** (Cockspur St., tel. 020/7925–0077), on the triangular corner of Trafalgar Square, serves standard Tex-Mex fare.

NATIONAL MARITIME MUSEUM

Since Great Britain is an island nation, it's not surprising that the British have a respect for the sea. As the largest maritime museum in the world, this is the place to get the full story. Both the building (by Christopher Wren) and its location (in beautiful parkland by the Thames with views over London) are picture-perfect. Arriving by boat completes the maritime experience.

As you'd imagine, boats feature heavily here, and model makers are in paradise examining the vast collection of Lilliputian reproductions, particularly Captain Cook's *Endeavour*, which contains tiny sailors, barrels, and brooms. But larger-scale vessels are represented here, too. Structural sections of boats—from submarines to the first motor launch, which looks both futuristic and antique—are found throughout the museum, often with their controls. After a complete revamp, the museum is rather like walking in and out of boats of all shapes and sizes, both in their prime and rusted away. Royal barges, for instance, evoke a romantic, gilded, Venetian-style era, when important people traveled by river from

EATS FOR KIDS

The nautically styled **restaurant** has a terrace and views of Greenwich Park. The changing menu features meat, fish, and vegetarian options, and kid's portions are generally available on request. A special kids' picnic area in the museum is outfitted submarine style.

KEEP IN MIND If you're planning to visit the *Cutty Sark* and the Royal Observatory (*see listings*), assuming you have enough energy, then the Greenwich Passport ticket makes sense. At £12 per adult, it's valid for two days plus a repeat visit within one year of purchase. A combination ticket to the museum and the observatory is £10.50 per adult.

 Romney Rd., Greenwich, SE10.
Tube: Greenwich

 £7.50 ages 17 and up

 Daily 10–5

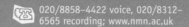 020/8858–4422 voice, 020/8312–6565 recording; www.nmn.ac.uk

 9 and up

palace to palace. If you're not sure what to see first, head to the Search Station, at the entrance, which covers treasures on display and still in storage.

Great seafaring heroes are given lots of space, from the swashbuckling explorer Francis Drake and the battle-scarred Nelson to the courageous polar explorer Captain Scott. On the more comfortable side, luxurious ocean-liner reconstructions give the flavor of grand voyages, and you can visit the wreck of the *Titanic* via screen and sound. Computers dot the galleries and supply information in greater depth.

The All Hands (on deck) area should be your final stop, both because it's more fun for kids after they've learned a little and because it's tough to drag them away (parents, too). Here they can steer a Viking ship (terribly difficult), navigate a Seacat into the channel, load a cargo vessel, and handle a ship's wheel—true hands-on deck experiences.

HEY, KIDS! Maritime doesn't just mean having to do with boats and navigation; it means having to do with the sea. The ocean is one of the world's great resources: 97% of the planet's water is stored in the oceans, of which we use around 1%. On your way out of the museum, look at the Sphere, in the glass-covered courtyard, and think a little about humans' role in preserving the fragile balance of life.

NATIONAL PORTRAIT GALLERY

You might be forgiven for missing the small entrance just around the corner from the grand columned entrance of the National Gallery, but you really shouldn't miss this museum, with the world's largest collection of portraits—both painted and photographic. It used to be a fairly dark and dingy place, rather like some of the somber portraits of England's early kings and queens. However, eager to join the string of galleries that have updated their interiors for the new millennium, the NPG has had a bold face-lift.

Looking at pictures of people, especially famous people, generally pleases kids, but the gallery also offers activities for children to make more of what they see—literally. Pick up a knapsack from the information desk; it's filled with ideas of things kids 7 and up can do with older siblings or parents. They can copy portraits with fuzzy felt, match fabric swatches with designs they spot in the paintings, or make a flamboyant mustache like those in some Victorian Gallery portraits. Also check at the information desk for special events and workshops (including photography), generally scheduled during school vacations.

EATS FOR KIDS The **Portrait Restaurant** (tel. 020/7312–2490) is run by a top London chef, and the ambience, view, and food are quite something. Down a level or two, in the basement next to the excellent bookshop, the **Portrait Café** is a more convenient stop for soups and sandwiches. Just opposite the gallery, **Café in the Crypt** (St. Martin-in-the-Fields, tel. 020/7839–4342) offers a hot budget lunch or salad bar, and you can tie that in with a free lunchtime chamber concert in the church (Tuesday and Thursday at 1:05), to soothe your soul as well your body. Also see the Brass Rubbing Centre.

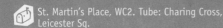

An escalator takes you on a chronological ride from the early 1400s on up. Pause to see the momentous paintings, particularly Holbein's full-length Henry VIII, whose girth would easily fill most galleries. Elizabeth I is immortalized with her heroes Walter Raleigh and Francis Drake. If period style is not to your taste, zoom on up to the Balcony Gallery for famous faces from the 1950s to the 1990s, including Princess Diana, Winston Churchill, Liz Taylor, and Paul McCartney, and artists like Hockney and Warhol, sometimes more famous than their subjects.

Still farther up, at the viewing area of the Portrait Restaurant, you'll get a panoramic view of a hero immortalized not on canvas but in stone—Lord Admiral Nelson among the pigeons of Trafalgar Square—and the Houses of Parliament, where many of the subjects in the gallery once held sway.

KEEP IN MIND
It's a good idea to call ahead for details about the special free children's and family activities (tel. 020/7312–2483).

HEY, KIDS! Look for the portrait of Nell Gwyn in the 17th- and 18th-century gallery on the second floor. A beautiful actress who started her career as an orange seller, she became more famous as the longtime mistress of Charles II than for her acting at the nearby Theatre Royal, on Drury Lane. The original version of this famous old London theater dated from 1663, but it burned down twice. Today's incarnation, completed in 1812, contains a huge auditorium that stages blockbuster musicals.

NATURAL HISTORY MUSEUM

Inspired by Fingal's Cave in wildest Scotland, the huge arches and spires of the Natural History Museum's grand facade give a hint of what's to be discovered in this amazing place bursting with wonders. At the main entrance, a diplodocus skeleton—so long it practically takes up the entire hall—greets you face to face. From here you can take any of the corridors that tail off into this vast museum, its acreage matched only by the British Museum's. Be warned, though. If you covered the entire museum, you'd likely become fossilized yourself, so be selective.

Among the Life Galleries, most kids' favorite exhibit is the dinosaurs, which you can reach by following the Waterhouse Way. (Alfred Waterhouse was the museum's master Victorian architect.) Here you can almost rub shoulders with the stars of *Jurassic Park*. A suspended walkway gets you a close look, and at its end, a lifelike feeding frenzy of ferocious hunters, complete with gory sound effects, attack a stray from the herd. (Younger kids might find this too scary.) A new lifelike T-Rex even has a virtual dung smell.

EATS FOR KIDS Kids with monster appetites find plenty at the **Life Galleries Restaurant,** by the dinosaur exhibit. Hot lunches include penne pasta and chicken nuggets (£2.95–£5.95). Cold eats and kids' lunch boxes are £3. By the Earth Galleries, the **Global Fast Food Café** has eat-and-go sandwiches and snacks.

KEEP IN MIND At Investigate, kids can really get their hands on the museum's hoard of ancient bones, skin, teeth, preserved bugs, and more. Friendly helpers show you how to weigh, measure, magnify, and discover more on computer about how these treasures fit into the circle of life. There's a worm world to watch behind glass, and myriad insects, not even visible to the naked eye, to gaze at under the microscope.

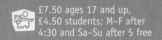 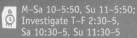 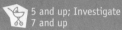

Cromwell Rd., SW7. Tube: South Kensington

020/7942-5000; www.nhm.ac.uk

£7.50 ages 17 and up, £4.50 students; M–F after 4:30 and Sa–Su after 5 free

M–Sa 10–5:50, Su 11–5:50; Investigate T–F 2:30–5, Sa 10:30–5, Su 11:30–5

5 and up; Investigate 7 and up

Arthropods were around before dinosaurs, and they are introduced, in larger-than-life form, in the creepy-crawlies exhibit in Room 33. A look around the mock kitchen and its uninvited visitors at No. 1 Crawley House is guaranteed to repulse—washcloths and garbage teeming with bugs, and you don't even want to know what's on the food. For older kids, the human biology exhibit in Room 22 shows what we're made of and how we survive; stand in the unborn baby and womb exhibit for a sense of life before birth.

Other wonders await in the Earth Galleries. On your way here, you can touch objects that mark evolution itself: massive mollusk shells, whales' teeth, and beautiful million-year-old rocks. Simulations and sets demonstrate the Earth's more spectacular restless movements, such as a video taken during the earthquake at Kobe, Japan, in which a supermarket floor shakes beneath you. Older kids like the Earth Lab, where they can use fossils and precious rocks, with the aid of museum scientists, to discover secrets of the Earth beneath their feet.

HEY, KIDS! Cheese skippers sound pretty tasty, but don't be mistaken. They're not some exciting new crunchy snack in a bag, but rather what you might find if cheese flying maggots have transformed your favorite lump of cheese into a nice, cozy nursery. And there are plenty of other tiny bugs on the menu in the creepy crawlies exhibit, ready to make a happy home in your kitchen.

REGENT'S CANAL

From Little Venice to Camden, a beautiful stretch of the Regent's Canal is one of London's best-kept secrets. Cutting through the leafy northern section of Regent's Park and at times almost invisible from the busy roads above, the canal is its own tranquil world. Willows trail in the gently lapping water, waterbirds buzz about their business, and stately herons stand still as statues. Private palatial gardens sweep down to the water at Regent's Park, and the charming little backyards of Camden's tall houses come with their own bobbing rowboats.

The easiest way to explore is on a tour given by Jason Canal Boats, out of Little Venice. From the elegant stucco houses that overlook the canal and little basin (marina), it's easy to see how this oasis got its name. The tiny tree-filled Browning Island, named after the poet Robert Browning, who lived within sight, is lined with gaily painted houseboats, which also appear at other basins farther along the canal. The *Jason* is similarly rigged out. Once inside, you can well imagine how compact you'd have to be to live in one.

KEEP IN MIND The London Waterbus Company (tel. 020/7482–2550 voice, 020/7482 2660 recording) connects Camden Lock and Little Venice, stopping at the London Zoo (zoo admission available at waterbus office, Camden Lock). Hourly service runs daily April–October, weekends November–March. To enjoy the canal for free, walk the towpath, open dawn–dusk. The prettiest part is from Camden Lock to Prince Albert Bridge, where you can access Regent's Park. For a nontourist route, go east from Camden Lock to picturesque St. Pancras Lock, where you can take the bridge to Euston Road and St. Pancras station, near the British Library.

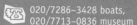
Jason Canal Boats, Blomfield Rd., W9.
Tube: Warwick Ave. London Canal Museum
12–13 New Wharf Rd., N1. Tube: King's
Cross

020/7286–3428 boats,
020/7713–0836 museum

Boat trips £5.95 round-
trip, museum £2.50
ages 19 and up, £1.25
children 9–18

Apr–Sept, daily 10:30, 12:30, 2:30, plus
4:30 Sa–Su June–Aug; Oct, daily 12:30,
2:30; museum T–Su 10–4:30

All ages

A guide provides lively commentary along the 45-minute nonstop ride. One of the highlights is passing through part of the London Zoo, where you can get a bird's-eye view of the Snowdon Aviary, see an antelope or two ambling about, and catch a whiff of the giraffe house. Among the historical anecdotes, you discover that the canal was a working route, where boats laden with goods were pulled along the towpath by horses. At a tunnel, the horses were unhitched and the boatmen had to "leg" through it, laying across the boat and "walking" along the tunnel sides. (If this fascinates you, discover more by legging it to the London Canal Museum, along the canal's eastern stretch.)

Above the towpath at Camden Lock and journey's end, a marketplace teems with life. Craft shops and trendy fashion stalls are a mecca for teens and twentysomethings, a marked contrast to the gentle lull of life below the bridge.

HEY, KIDS! The Queen owns some of the palatial mansions at the boundary of Regent's Park. These are rented out for a fortune, and their gardens, which slope down to the canal, are second in size only to Buckingham Palace—now that's big!

EATS FOR KIDS Jason's Restaurant, canalside, has a set two-course lunch Monday–Thursday. Crisps (potato chips) and drinks are sold on the boat. Red Pepper (8 Formosa St., tel. 020/7266–2708) is a jolly pizzeria where kids can play with dough while lunch cooks. The pizzas are large, so kids can share. By Camden Lock, Sauce Diner (214 Camden High St., tel. 020/7482–0777) has all-organic, fresh food. Veggie and beef burgers, grilled pork, and chicken feature on the children's menu, baked chicken, king prawns, and rib-eye steak on the parents'. Smoothies and desserts are mouthwatering.

REGENT'S PARK

Probably the most perfect of London's parks, the 18th-century Regent's Park was designed by John Nash for the Prince Regent. The elegant terraces of grand houses sweep the Outer Circle's perimeter and buffer this haven from traffic noise. An Inner Circle connects many recreational areas, too, such as open spaces for playing (you might find a baseball game to crash), playgrounds, fragrant flower gardens, a boating lake, and an open-air theater.

Start from York Gate, between the Regent's Park and Baker Street tubes, where York Bridge leads to the Inner Circle and the gilded gates to Queen Mary's Gardens. Come to this stunning floral epicenter in June, and you'll reel with the scent of the magnificent rose garden and its laden swags and pillars. Traipse across the Japanese bridge (if it's not blocked by a posing bridal party) to discover a cascade and duck island in a little lake. Look carefully, and you may see a "posing" heron. Also nearby are another waterfall and fountains with tiny pergola "secret" gardens. If you time it right, you can see a children's play at the

KEEP IN MIND

Primrose Hill, to the north, on the far side of the Regent's Canal and Prince Albert Road, is nevertheless a part of Regent's Park. Climb up to its grassy hilltop, and you'll be rewarded with a superb panorama of the park and the London skyline.

EATS FOR KIDS **Park Cafés** are situated across the park: the one at Queen Mary's Gardens has the largest menu, often with seasonal choices of pasta, chicken, soup, salads, and snacks; in summer, eat alfresco surrounded by roses. The slightly smaller chalet-style café, on the Broad Walk, also has a varied menu, featuring delicious soups and sticky pastries. At the boating lake and playgrounds, **kiosks** sell sandwiches, ices, and drinks. Alternatively, buy picnic fixings from **Marks & Spencer** (*see* London Zoo) if coming via Camden Town tube, or **Pret a Manger** (120 Baker St., tel. 020/7486–2264) if arriving via Baker Street tube. Also see London Planetarium and Madame Tussaud's.

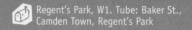
Regent's Park, W1. Tube: Baker St.,
Camden Town, Regent's Park

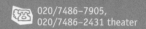
020/7486–7905,
020/7486–2431 theater

Free

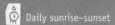
Daily sunrise–sunset

All ages

open-air theater (open June–September). Shakespeare's *A Midsummer Night's Dream* never had a more perfect setting, except when it rains.

Outside the Inner Circle (almost where you started) is a lake where you can rent a rowboat for an hour and navigate around a wildfowl island. Paddleboats are smaller but just as much fun. For more action, kids can bounce around in one of three playgrounds. Maps are posted at many entrances, or get one from the Information Centre, at the east end of the Inner Circle, by Chester Road.

Peer through the railings of the London Zoo (*see above*), and see some of the animals for free. A camel, elephants, exotic birds, and an occasional roaring lion are on the left side of the zoo, the wolf wood is to the right, and giraffes are opposite the entrance. For smaller wildlife, visit the leafy canalside (*see* Regent's Canal), where barges ferry visitors from Camden Lock to Little Venice and back—but that's another trip.

HEY, KIDS! As you walk among the beautiful landscaped lawns and formal flower beds, watch your step. During World War II, the park was used by the military, and no fewer than 300 bombs (including V2 rockets) fell on the grounds. The once undulating land was flattened by infilling with dumped bomb rubble. Even today (though not very often, so don't worry too much), the ground can cave in where the fill is loose and where there are pockets or old air-raid shelters.

ROCK CIRCUS

Ready to stand eyeball to eyeball with pop stars from the '50s to the present? From skiffle to heavy metal, bop to hip-hop, this museum of waxworks and memorabilia takes you on a rock-history tour, with music, lights, and atmospheric noise every step of the way. Though kids' favorites tend to be current, parents enjoy a trip down memory lane.

Allow about two hours to take in all the sets, from the weirdness of Michael Jackson to the teen highlight: the pre-concert VIP area, where you can hang out with the stars. Watch Madonna on video, check out the Spice Girls' and other pop stars' clothes in the Memorabilia Corridor, and groove along with Jon Bon Jovi at the Stadium Gig. Often you find yourself wandering around the models as if you're part of the action.

Parents tend to be fascinated by the early stuff, wondering, for instance, how the Beatles became so big with such a basic drum kit. The emphasis is rightly on the legends, and kids can see how current music and style have developed over the decades. It's hard not to realize

EATS FOR KIDS While Gloria Estefan and other stars wind down at the After Show Party, you can wind down at the nearby **café,** offering coffee, fizzy drinks, crisps (chips), and candy. **Planet Hollywood** (13 Coventry St., tel. 020/7287–1000) serves terrific burgers amid movie-star memorabilia, but prices are high. For a wide range of wild food— Mojo Bones, Wiki-Wiki Wings, Wallaby's Wok—bushwack to the **Rainforest Café** (20 Shaftesbury Ave., tel. 020/7434–3111), behind Piccadilly Circus. Dishes are pricey, but the entertainment—roaring fake furry animals, thunderstorms, waterfalls, and real tropical fish—are free. Kids love it, but beware the well-stocked shop.

London Pavilion, Piccadilly Circus, W1. Tube: Leicester Sq., Piccadilly Circus

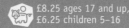
£8.25 ages 17 and up, £6.25 children 5–16

020/7734-7203; www.rock-circus.com

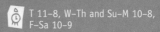
T 11–8, W–Th and Su–M 10–8, F–Sa 10–9

10 and up

that very little is totally new. As music evolves, it tends to recycle itself—rather like the hip clothes of the 1970s that became all the rage again in the late '90s.

In the spooky Cemetery section, the dead look alive, as real as the graves themselves. Marc Bolan of T.Rex plays guitar perched on his tombstone, and Michael Hutchence of INXS seems to stand before you, with an interview going on in the background.

You can browse through various street scenes, including a London street in the swinging '60s, a music store in the early Bob Dylan era, and a very cheeky shop called Sex, run by punk royals Malcolm McLaren and Vivienne Westwood. Wall-mounted CD players throughout let you listen to music across the eras, and the Rock and Pop Shop gives ample opportunity to buy. But the really cool souvenir is a photo of you with your favorite rock idol.

HEY, KIDS! It takes about six months from the star's first sitting to make a waxwork figure. The final cost comes to a cool £30,000. The hair is real (even the underarm stuff) and is washed and spruced up regularly.

KEEP IN MIND Younger kids might find some of the loud noises a little frightening, and there is very little on rap, dance, and the current pop girl and boy bands. But if you steer your kids a little, they'll find they can put the current chart hits in context.

ROYAL BOTANIC GARDENS

There's a whole different kind of kingdom to explore at Kew—the plant kingdom. Here on 300 pretty, peaceful acres, plants from throughout the world and the ages can be seen and discovered.

In 1759, the Princess of Wales, Augusta, started the gardens with a botanic collection near the Orangery, on the grounds of Kew Palace. The collection and grounds grew, and wonderful garden buildings, such as the Chinese Pagoda, sprang up. Built as a surprise for the princess, at 10 stories of red-gray brick, the pagoda must have been some surprise. You can't miss it, even from outside the garden walls. Other fabulous buildings followed. The huge Temperate House and Palm House, by Decimus Burton (of Hyde Park Arch fame), are lovely. Elevated areas let you climb up around the palms, and a marine section contains giant kelp, used in lipstick, toothpaste, and ice cream. (With a potential length of 100 meters—over 300 feet—it must be kept under control.) Bananas grow in the Palm House, as do cocoa trees, giant bamboo, and tropical rain-forest plants, such as

EATS FOR KIDS **Café al Fresco** has a lovely outdoor terrace on which to eat in summer, but when it's colder, inside is good, too. Like the gardens, the menu reflects the seasons: in summer, salads and barbecued meats, warming vegetable soups—such as pumpkin—in autumn.

KEEP IN MIND Make the visitor center your first stop to stock up on useful maps and leaflets. Specially for children, the "Kids' Kew" leaflet has a list of plants to hunt for, background on the various buildings, and fun facts on the fascinating flora. Grown-ups visiting in summer might want to stay for the evening jazz concert series. Kids enjoy the relaxing atmosphere and the fireworks displays. (These may not occur on every night of the jazz fest, so check beforehand.)

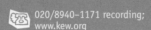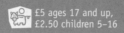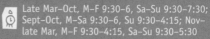

Kew Rd., Richmond. Tube: Kew Gardens. Rail: Kew Bridge

020/8940–1171 recording; www.kew.org

£5 ages 17 and up, £2.50 children 5–16

Late Mar–Oct, M–F 9:30–6, Sa–Su 9:30–7:30; Sept–Oct, M–Sa 9:30–6, Su 9:30–4:15; Nov–late Mar, M–F 9:30–4:15, Sa–Su 9:30–5:30

All ages

the super-climber Hairy Mary. You can see the ancient cycad, around when dinosaurs roamed.

The incredible role of plants in the circle of life is explored in the Evolution House, which contains fossils of early ferns. If dramatic and exotic is your thing, walk across the world's climatic zones in the Princess of Wales Conservatory; here you see prickly cacti, giant water lilies to rival Monet's, the carnivorous Venus's flytrap, and bizarre plants that pose as stones to avoid being eaten.

And that's just the indoor stuff. The buildings are mere dots on this broad landscape of interlinked formal gardens, arboretums, and woodland on the River Thames. You can run or meander, and as the seasons change, so does the scenery. Early spring brings carpets of purple crocuses; late spring sees trees laden with cherry blossoms. Summer is the time for the scent of roses and blooming water lilies as well as fun kid activities that emphasize eco-friendliness. A garden is always full of surprises.

HEY, KIDS! The Venus's flytrap, that most enterprising of plants, can also count. It efficiently snaps up its prey—flies and other small insects—when it has felt not one but two touches on the fine hairs inside its leaves. If you're lucky enough to see one of these amazing plants in action in the Princess of Wales Conservatory, you'll also discover that its fly-catching maneuver makes it the planet's plant sprint champ.

ROYAL MEWS AT BUCKINGHAM PALACE

The Queen's palace is London's most stately sight, with guards standing sentry inside the ornate black-and-gold gates (*see* Changing of the Guard). But equally impressive are the gilded coaches and elegant black carriages that sweep out majestically along the Mall with their horses and liveried coachmen on state and royal occasions. These glorious coaches are kept in the stable courtyard, or mews, at the side of the palace and can be seen along with some tack and the horses themselves.

The first stage of your visit passes the Riding School, where the horses are trained. It's a rigorous program, which includes pulling broad, heavy weights and learning to keep cool while bands play and crowds wave flags and shout. Queen Victoria's young family of nine was schooled in riding here, but not the current princes William and Harry.

Next come the carriages, stationed outside each numbered door. They are decked in highly polished leather, red and gilt paint, and shiny brass lanterns and are quite high off the

KEEP IN MIND The State Rooms at Buckingham Palace are only open to the public when the Queen is out of town in the summer. In the main, this is during July and August. Tickets should be booked a month in advance by calling the visitor center number above. It's worth noting that although the decor and treasures on display are undoubtedly amazing for adults, they don't tend to interest kids as much.

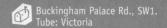
Buckingham Palace Rd., SW1.
Tube: Victoria

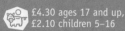
£4.30 ages 17 and up,
£2.10 children 5–16

M–Th 10:30–4:30

020/7839–1377 or 020/7321–2233;
www.royalcollection.org.uk

5 and up

ground. So how does the Queen ascend regally? A swift response comes from one of the stewards: a footman unfolds steps from inside the carriage door. The Gold State Coach is the must-see masterpiece, almost completely gold with cherubs and two mythical Tritons on the back to scare off anyone racing up behind. These stately vehicles don't race, however. They proceed at walking pace, pulled by four pairs of horses with postilion riders and accompanying footmen, all in red-and-gold regalia. The Queen used the coach for her 1952 coronation and 1977 Silver Jubilee. It's sure to be a sight at the Golden Jubilee in 2002.

It's unlikely you'll catch the Queen in the stables, although she does name each horse herself. Her Majesty is an accomplished rider, and the beautiful little saddles used by the young Princesses Elizabeth and Margaret are on exhibit in the Harness Room. One is decorated with flowers; if you look close up, you'll see they are little shells sewn together.

HEY, KIDS! If you were wondering what the word "mews" means, it is from the French word "*mue*," which means to shed an outer coat, or moult. In days of old, the word was used for the place where falcons were kept when they were shedding their feathers.

EATS FOR KIDS Head towards Victoria Street rather than Buckingham Palace Road for a better selection of coffee bars, such as **Starbucks** (137 Victoria St., tel. 020/7233–5170). The excellent **Spaghetti House** (3 Bressenden Pl., tel. 020/7834–5650) serves truly Italian pasta, pizza, and meat dishes in a friendly modern bistro setting. Smaller portions at reduced prices are available for kids.

ROYAL NATIONAL THEATRE

Here's a chance for young drama enthusiasts to go behind the scenes of one of Britain's most famous theaters—to see how it all works and learn the tricks of the trade. You never know what might happen; you might even brush past a great actor as you pass the dressing rooms.

A guide with an encyclopedic knowledge of plays past and forthcoming takes you into each of the three theaters that make up the National Theatre complex and explains the mechanics of each. Sitting in each one, perhaps catching part of a rehearsal, you discover how each one's shape and size suit varying performances.

Backstage areas are like vast warehouses. You see entire sets ready to be wheeled in and out, just like freight on rail tracks. Countless props and furniture pieces—even glitzy chandeliers dangling high in the rafters—are recycled time and again. Not only can you peek at the props, but you learn how they work and how they're made and hear fascinating

KEEP IN MIND In addition to the permanent theater-history exhibition in the Olivier Theatre, there are changing exhibitions of art and craft in the vast foyer area. Throughout the summer, dance, mime, and music events are staged on the open-air riverside walk just outside the theater—all for free.

HEY, KIDS! Even the most clever stage props can go wrong. In one performance of *Peter Pan*, Smee, the pirate cook, had to improvise quickly when Captain Hook's hook shot out suddenly into the audience. He retrieved it. And in a grisly scene from *Macbeth*, a fake bloodied head was not made heavy enough. It ended up bouncing, like a ball, across the stage.

South Bank Centre, SE1.
Tube: Waterloo

Free; backstage tour £4.75

M–Sa 3 times a day; times vary
based on performances

020/7452–3400;
www.nt-online.org

8 and up

tales about their stage successes and disasters. For instance, you find out why there are three different huge, but almost cuddly, working crocodiles needed in *Peter Pan* and how the fake food for *Wind in the Willows* is made to look good enough to eat. (The Theatre Museum has an exhibition devoted to this production; *see below.*) You even discover the secrets of how real-looking blood is made to spurt out at just the right second—well, sometimes it's been hit or miss. In the scenery-making area, you see the genius of the stage designers, who turn bits of seeming garbage into realistic-looking sets. Green painted raffia becomes stage grass; hard sponge turns to stone. You might even wonder if it's the set designers, rather than the actors, who are the real masters of disguise.

At tour's end, you can follow a time line on the history of the theater, but more likely you'll be itching to reserve seats for the next sizzling performance, so you can see all that backroom work from the front.

EATS FOR KIDS   The theater contains **Mezzanine** (tel. 020/7452–3600), for fine dining; the **Terrace Café** (tel. 020/7452–3555), with grills, salads, and pasta; and the **Circle Cafe,** with the most family appeal. They open based on performances. **EAT** espresso bar has great coffee, pastries, and outdoor tables. **LyHelton Beffet** has sandwiches and sweets. The People's Palace (Level 3, Royal Festival Hall, tel. 020/7928–9999) *is* a chic restaurant next door, and La Barca (81 Lower Marsh, tel. 020/7261–9221) *is* a cozy trattoria.

ROYAL OBSERVATORY

18

It's about time. The Greenwich observatory is synonymous with time and its connection with the Earth and sea. The world's timekeeping system, Greenwich Mean Time, and those thin black horizontal and vertical lines, latitude and longitude, were derived here through laborious work by royal astronomers (0° longitude passes through Greenwich). Pause in the observatory courtyard to see the actual meridian—a brass line across the cobbles. A photo, legs astride the western and eastern hemispheres, is a must.

The small museum traces the history of astronomy and the search for navigational longitude. It's an absorbing place, and though far from interactive, it still interests kids who love planets, seafaring, and timekeeping. There are telescopes, clocks, chronometers, and other exquisite historical timepieces as well as exhibits charting discoveries by distinguished royal astronomers, such as John Flamsteed, after whom the building (designed by Christopher Wren) is named, and Edmund Halley, of comet fame. But it wasn't until John Harrison that an accurate clock was made to measure longitude; his sea clocks, H-1 to

HEY, KIDS! The red ball on top of the observatory drops down the rod at 1 PM on the dot, the same as every day since 1833. Sailors used this system to set their clocks precisely to Greenwich Mean Time. Before then, the sun and stars were used to measure latitude, but without an accurate onboard clock, they couldn't determine their longitude. And without that knowledge, many a ship came to a horrible end, unable to find its destination precisely or on schedule. Boats were shipwrecked and crews starved all because sailors couldn't determine time and longitude accurately enough.

Greenwich Park, SE10. Tube: Greenwich Maritime

020/8312-6575 voice, 020/8312-6565 recording, 020/8312-6608 planetarium; www.rog.nmn.ac.uk

Observatory £6 ages 16 and up; planetarium shows £2 ages 16 and up, £1.50 children 15 and under

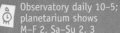
Observatory daily 10–5; planetarium shows M–F 2, Sa–Su 2, 3

10 and up

H-5, are here. To make sense of it all, visit the wall display and press the longitude lines to see how time changes around the world.

Too much street light and pollution forced the main Royal Observatory operations to move out of London, but you can still look through the camera obscura. With a small aperture in the roof, a mirror, a round table, and a completely dark room, it shows a 360° image of the outside world, in this case the National Maritime Museum (*see above*). You can watch a star show in the domed planetarium, and on scheduled dates you can look through the huge refracting telescope to view planets with the help of an astronomer. On most Tuesday afternoons, you can look through a smaller modern reflecting telescope in the courtyard, but do call ahead to check times. Speaking of checking times, as you leave the observatory, don't forget to check your watch by the grand old 24-hour clock still ticking away.

KEEP IN MIND A discounted, combination ticket for the National Maritime Museum and the Royal Observatory costs £10.50 for adults. The Greenwich Passport ticket (£12 per adult) includes the *Cutty Sark* and is valid for two days and another repeat visit within one year of purchase.

EATS FOR KIDS If you don't want to go far, just opposite the observatory, the **Park Café** (*see* Greenwich Park) is your best choice. If you have a combination ticket with the National Maritime Museum (*see above*), you may want to eat in its **restaurant**. Another option is to browse around Greenwich center (*see Cutty Sark*) and see what you like.

ST. PAUL'S CATHEDRAL

Hard to believe, but this is the watered-down version of Christopher Wren's original design for rebuilding the old St. Paul's, after its destruction in the Great Fire of 1666. The stunning cathedral has been the scene of huge ceremony, such as the wedding of Diana to Prince Charles.

Before walking up the sweeping steps to the main door, go to the crypt on the left, where an excellent shop sells a fun children's guidebook, featuring games alongside the key facts. It highlights the important stops, including the tombs of Lord Nelson and Wren himself, who didn't live to see his great work finished. His Latin memorial states: "If you ask for his monument, look around you." The somber granite sarcophagus of the Duke of Wellington is here, too, while his large memorial is in the nave.

Check out the beautiful ceilings, particularly above the quire (choir) and high altar, where glinting, brightly colored mosaics show heavenly images. Wren churches display

HEY, KIDS!
While creating the dome murals, the artist Thornhill stepped back from his rope platform to admire his work and almost fell off, but his quick-thinking assistant grabbed him in time. Though it left a blotch, a life was saved. Can you spot where?

EATS FOR KIDS Beneath the beautiful arches, the **Crypt Café** offers a children's menu with mozzarella pizza or chicken fingers with ice cream and drink for £4.25. Smart choices for adults include a chicken niçoise salad (with olives and anchovies) and herbed haddock fish cakes with vegetable sides (allow around £10). For french fries in a French-style bar-bistro and substantial steak or chicken baguettes that children can share (from £6.95), try the aptly named **Café Dôme** (4 St. Paul's Churchyard, tel. 020/7489–0767). Opposite the cathedral, it has a wonderful view of the facade.

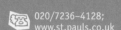
St. Paul's Churchyard, EC4.
Tube: Cannon St., St. Paul's

020/7236-4128;
www.st.pauls.co.uk

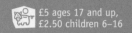
£5 ages 17 and up,
£2.50 children 6–16

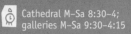
Cathedral M–Sa 8:30–4;
galleries M–Sa 9:30–4:15

5 and up

spacious, clean simplicity with sudden bursts of decoration in just the right place (a stark contrast to the more ornate and overstuffed Westminster Abbey). Behind the altar is the American Chapel, commemorating GIs killed in the war.

The dome is the big attraction, literally, its walls painted with sepia murals of St. Paul. To look closer, climb the many stairs to the Whispering Gallery, around the dome's circumference. Stand against the wall a distance away from someone, and play the popular whispering game. You can hear your words echo, hopefully distinguishing your message from everyone else's. For the ultimate stair-climbing challenge—650 steps total—and assuming you have a head for heights, climb the slightly scary, spiralling grated stairs even farther to the Golden Gallery, outside the top of the dome. The matchless view stretches for miles, taking in the Monument to the Great Fire; the river bend that makes Big Ben look as if it's leaped to the South Bank; the Tate Modern, a monster redbrick building (very un-Wren); and the Millennium Bridge, a graceful steel curve that leads back to St. Paul's.

KEEP IN MIND You'll need strong, stable shoes for walking up to the Whispering Gallery, and strong, stable legs and nerves to attempt the stairs to the balustrade outside the dome. The Triforium Tour takes you to parts of the cathedral not open to the public with general admission, including the library, Wren's great model of the cathedral, and another bunch of stairs: the Geometrical (or Dean's) Staircase. This tour runs on Mondays and Thursdays and costs £10, including cathedral admission.

SCIENCE MUSEUM

E yes and minds open wide in this museum's new, souped-up Wellcome Wing, which opened in summer 2000. The wing is undeniably cool, with blue lighting and a sci-fi lab atmosphere, but what makes it—and the rest of the museum, for that matter—even cooler is that the hands-on exhibits here are related to everyday things. After a visit, kids won't think of science as just space travel and DNA.

There are over 800 exhibits to try here, so physical and mental stamina (not to mention a lot of time) are musts. Head for one of the touch-screen terminals located by the main stairs and elevators for suggested itineraries (e.g., In a Hurry for Families and What to Do in Two Hours or Less). Or just stay in the Wellcome Wing. The tiniest visitors can learn how basic science works at Launch Pad, where they can press, push, pull, or play with sand and water while learning about light, sound, and electricity. Older kids (around 10–

HEY, KIDS! Next time you miss a day at school, why not pick up a few new excuses from the Who Am I? exhibit, which explores some of the strange genetic diseases you just may have inherited—for the day? You could try fooling your friends that you had a tiny case of didaskaleinophobia, and see if they know the meaning (a fear of going to school). Or how about decidophobia (a fear of making decisions)? And as for the dreaded visit to the dentist, well there's always a sudden instance of iatrophobia.

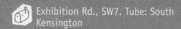 Exhibition Rd., SW7. Tube: South
Kensington

 0870/870-4868;
www.sciencemuseum.org.uk

 £6.95 ages 17 and up, after 4:30
free; IMAX £6.96 ages 17 and up,
£5.75 children 5–16; both £12
ages 17 and up

 Daily 10–6

 3 and up

13) like the In the Future gallery, where computers let them enter their opinions about such topics as picking the sex of your child, men having babies, holidays in space, and growing young, and then find out what other kids think. Children of all ages enjoy the 3-D IMAX presentations, in which you get to wear those funny specs and perceive things (like the moon's surface) as if you are really there.

Exploring genetics is a slightly more challenging subject, yet again interactive exhibits help make the learning fun. It's all part of everyone's favorite subject—themselves—in the Who Am I? exhibit. Discover how you got those distinguishing features, and, if you want, become part of actual scientific research in Live Science. But then that's the whole point of a visit here—to discover how we live through the eyes of science.

KEEP IN MIND
To help you plan your itinerary, notice the hand symbols on the museum map (indicating hands-on galleries) as well as the times of demonstrations, performances, and workshops. Note that children under 12 must be accompanied by an adult in the Launch Pad.

EATS FOR KIDS As you will be much too busy exploring and inter-acting to leave the museum, you might as well plunge into the high-tech-design **Deep Blue Café,** on the ground floor. A children's menu consists of chicken nuggets, minipizza, or pasta plus dessert and drink, and other options are rotisserie chicken and fries, pizzas, and salads. The self-serve **Museum Café** sells lunch and snack in less-chic surroundings, and the **Eat Drink Shop** is basic self-serve with hot dogs, sandwiches, cakes, ices, and candy bars.

SHAKESPEARE'S GLOBE

On the bank of the Thames, under bundles of water reeds, and surrounded by English oak, William Shakespeare's artistic home has risen again. The Globe was the persistent dream of the late Sam Wanamaker, who tried to find Shakespeare's London theater as a young actor in 1949. All that was left of it then was a plaque in a pub, but through his efforts, the Globe was reborn just a few hundred yards from its original foundations and a few centuries after its 1600s heyday.

From the moment you walk into the open-air theater, you enter a time warp. As tour guides explain, few concessions to modern technology were made in its construction. Everything was done by hand, without electricity, as in Shakespeare's day; look hard, there is not a screw in sight. Those water reeds make the only thatched roof in London, as they were banned after the Great Fire. Oak forms the supports, seats, and stage. Performances are authentic, too, with no microphones or lighting. Music is provided by lutes, pipes, drums, and other instruments of the time—you can see them in the exhibit (*see below*)—

HEY, KIDS!
The Globe is shaped like a wooden "O." If you pay more for a ticket, you can sit underneath the circular thatched roof. The audience in the center, called the groundlings, have no roof. If it rains, yes, they get wet, and the show goes on.

KEEP IN MIND If you want to get a taste for the real thing—and perhaps be a groundling—attend one of several matinees during the summer Shakespeare season. Running concurrently is ChildsPlay, the ultimate in cultural baby-sitting. While parents enjoy a full play, their children attend this workshop (£9), which zooms in on bite-size sections of the play and sparks kids' imaginations through drama, storytelling, and art. Kids then watch the last 20 minutes in the theater.

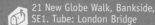
21 New Globe Walk, Bankside, SE1. Tube: London Bridge

020/77902-1500;
www.shakespeares-globe.org

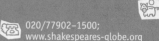
£7.50 ages 16 and up, £6 students, £7 children 5-15; performances: groundlings £5, seats from £10 ages 16 and up, from £9 children

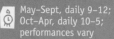
May-Sept, daily 9-12; Oct-Apr, daily 10-5; performances vary

8 and up

and musicians stroll from stage to audience as the play demands. When cannon fire was needed for *Henry V*, the *Golden Hinde* replica, just along the riverbank, obliged.

The largest exhibit of its kind in the world, Shakespeare's Globe Exhibition celebrates the Bard's plays—from Dame Judi Dench to Disney and including gorgeous handmade costumes. It also covers the drama of how craftsmen built the theater as well as archaeological finds—among them a child's tiny leather shoes and jerkin. Drawings, paintings, and diary entries show that Southwark (aka the South Bank), with its playhouses, alehouses, and bear dancing (Bear Gardens is next door), was London's playground in the days of the original Globe. When the Puritan regime closed the theater in 1644, the area died with it. Today, thanks to the Tate Modern and the Millennium Bridge, Southwark is enjoying a renaissance—something in which the late Sam Wanamaker played an immeasurable part.

EATS FOR KIDS The **Globe Café** (tel. 020/7902-1576) serves lunch, brunch, and snacks; sandwiches and soup are pricey, at £3.75 and £6.95, but they come with a beautiful view over the theater piazza and the Millennium Bridge and across the river to St Paul's Cathedral. For other dining suggestions, see *Golden Hinde*, *Tate Modern*, and *Millennium Bridge*.

SOMERSET HOUSE

One of London's best-kept architectural secrets, the magnificent riverside Somerset House has squeezed out the dreary offices that were once here and opened its front and back doors to the public. The front (Strand) entrance brings you to the Courtauld Gallery (*see above*), with its fine art collection; the back (Embankment) entrance leads to the Gilbert Collection of decorative arts. Between the two is a magnificent cobbled courtyard that almost feels like an Italian palazzo, and though the Courtauld and Gilbert Collection are well worth separate visits, the rest of Somerset House is a fun, beautiful place to spend an hour or two.

The most exciting way to arrive is by foot from Waterloo Bridge, from the south bank of the river. Try to imagine centuries ago, when the Thames, London's lifeblood, lapped at Somerset House's back entrance, and Navy Board barges carrying officers arrived from Greenwich. You can see the Navy Commissioners' Barge at the old river level, beneath the Great Arch, bearing the face of Old Father Thames. A huge video that plays on the

EATS FOR KIDS The **Admiralty Deli,** in Seaman's Hall, sells snacks and drinks to eat in the courtyard. To sit on the river terrace, you have to eat at the sophisticated, pricey **Admiralty** (tel. 020/7845–4646) restaurant. More fun is had on the far side of Covent Garden, at **Belgo** (50 Earlham St., tel. 020/7813–2233), a weird techno monastery (waiters wear funky Trappist monk outfits) where kids can color before plunging into fabulous Belgian frites (fries), with crumbed chicken or fish. Parents make do with mussels stuffed with different savory mixtures, washed down with fruity beers. See Courtauld Gallery and Covent Garden.

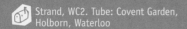
Strand, WC2. Tube: Covent Garden, Holborn, Waterloo

 Free

 M–Sa 10–6, Su 12–6

 020/7845-4600; www.somerset-house.org.uk

 6 and up

entrance-lobby wall tells the house's history, and around the corner, the education room hosts practical activities, such as mask making and other crafts. (Younger children must be accompanied by an adult.) For a thought-provoking self-guided tour, pick up a free family guide sheet, which gets you hunting around the river terrace, the restored Seaman's Hall, and the courtyard.

The courtyard is the hub for a huge range of activities on many weekends, particularly in summer: free music performances, mimes, and more to watch, plus children's art projects, such as scrap sculpture, and other crafts to join in for as little or as long as you want. A quarterly events sheet gives full details. While you watch today's activity, realize that beneath your feet lie the remains of the Tudor palace built by the Duke of Somerset. Just imagine how the royal jester might have entertained the future Queen Elizabeth I, who used to live here.

HEY, KIDS! Admiral Nelson, an important figure on the Navy Board, reported regularly to Somerset House. Although his character looms large, as the family guide sheet describes, he was actually "a thin, spare naval officer with only one arm . . . His thin, frail figure shook at every step."

KEEP IN MIND Drop-in workshops for children run 11:30–1 and 2–4; phone ahead for dates and details or check the "What's On" leaflet at the admission desk. Guided tours that include the Gilbert Collection (£6) run Tuesdays, Thursdays, and Saturdays at 1:30 and take 1 hour and 15 minutes; tours that include the Courtauld Gallery (£9) start at 3:15 on those same days. Guided walks (tel. 020/7514–5777) travel from the Museum of London past the river and include a tour of Somerset House (£7.50).

SYON PARK

Despite jets from nearby Heathrow airport rumbling overhead, Syon Park has acres of beautiful, peaceful gardens rolling down to the River Thames. Home of the dukes of Northumberland for over 400 years, Syon has had gardens since 1431, when it was a medieval abbey. When it became a ducal residence, the gardens were redesigned on a grand scale by Capability (Lancelot) Brown, the must-have gardener of the era.

As you enter, you come to the most eye-catching feature: the Great Conservatory. Made by Charles Fowler, who also designed the old flower market at Covent Garden, it is filled with plants, many of which have an interesting tale concerning their arrival from some exotic corner of the globe. Your kids might want to run from one end to the other or in circles around the pretty fountain in the garden behind. From here a path leads to the rose garden and Syon House itself. You can sneak a peek inside the grand entrance; even children are in awe of the gorgeous high decorated ceilings. While you stroll and breathe in the delicate scents of the rose garden, your kids can run between the beds.

HEY, KIDS!

Henry VIII's coffin lay here overnight on its way from Westminster to Windsor for burial, but in the morning the coffin was found open and dogs were licking the remains. Could it be divine retribution because Henry closed the abbey that once stood on the grounds?

KEEP IN MIND

On wet days, you might want to tour the splendid interior of Syon House, with its fabulous Robert Adam decor, but your children probably won't. They'll want to go to the indoor adventure playground, Snakes and Ladders (tel. 020/8847–0946), for tiny tots and young kids up to 10 (height limit of 4 feet 8 inches). It's open daily 10–6 and costs from £3.55 per child weekends, £2.85 weekdays. Also on the grounds of Syon Park are the Aquatic Experience and London Butterfly House (*see above* for both).

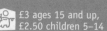

London Rd., Brentford.
Tube: Gunnersbury

020/8560-0881

£3 ages 15 and up,
£2.50 children 5–14

Daily 10–5:30, or sunset

3 and up

Around the conservatory, proud peacocks strut about, showing off their plumage—a great photo op—and warning you to keep your distance with their eerie shrieks. On weekends, you can catch a miniature steam railway, which trundles past a lake to Flora's Lawn, a lovely picnic and game-playing spot. On a pretty walk beside the lake you might see all sorts of ducks, their nests hidden in the reeds. Look out for many unusual types of tree, too. Syon has a diverse collection, and some, like the Indian bean, whose tangly trunk snakes along the ground, are a dream for kids to climb. Take the footbridge and path toward the tidal water meadows (also the site of a Civil War battle in 1642), and watch the Thames and its bobbing boats and chic waterside houses. It's hard to believe the city is just a short way from this idyllic place.

EATS FOR KIDS   Since it's quite a way to get off-site, you are pretty much a captive audience. The self-service **Patio Café,** at the park entrance, serves a wide range of child-friendly dishes (pasta, sausages, and chicken to name a few), snacks, and drinks. You can bring your own picnic to the park, but first fill your picnic bag at the **Syon Park Farm Shop,** near the parking lot, which has some unusual organic English produce and a good deli.

TATE BRITAIN

Just because the current fuss is about Tate Modern (and justifiably so—*see below*), downriver on Bankside, don't pass Tate Britain by. Now that the international pictures that were once here have emigrated to the South Bank, the greatest collection of British works anywhere can be seen in newly bright and spacious surroundings. The gallery has taken the bold step of arranging works thematically. So your family can walk into a room called The Portrait and enjoy wildly different styles from different centuries hanging in the same space. Compare the formal 18th-century painting of the *Bishop of Winchester*, by Hogarth, with Peter Blake's pioneering pop art *Self-Portrait with Badges*, from 1961. This juxtaposition continues throughout the gallery and covers other subjects, such as war, land, and home life. The result is a fun, new perspective on art.

Come on a Sunday afternoon, 2–5, when the kids' Art Trolley is wheeled out. From it, children can collect materials, head for a designated work (perhaps David Hockney's *Bigger Splash*), set themselves up on the floor, and make their own work of art. There are other activity

EATS FOR KIDS Few cafés are nearby, but there's enough here to satisfy. On-the-spot hot and cold snacks including sandwiches, sausages, baked potatoes, and baked beans can be had at the **Tate Café & Espresso Bar,** in the basement. **Tate Restaurant** (tel. 020/7887–8825) is the more grown-up and expensive option—but no less friendly for that. It's famous for its fine wine list and wall murals by Whistler. You can order reduced-price, smaller portions for kids from the main menu, which has a wide selection of fish and meat dishes.

 Millbank, SW1.
Tube: Pimlico

 Free

 Daily 10–5:50

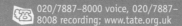 020/7887–8000 voice, 020/7887–8008 recording; www.tate.org.uk

 6 and up

choices, too, and the trolley is updated regularly to reflect the galleries' changing displays. Older kids often work quietly on their own, allowing you to take an uninterrupted look at the paintings by yourself without anyone getting frustrated.

The information desk dispenses audio guides as well as special kids' work sheets based on different themes, such as "Signs and Symbols," "Animal Antics," and "Something Old, Something New." Armed with pencil and clipboard, children head off for works around the gallery. Sheets get them to think about what is happening in each piece and to compare art from different times as well as suggest ways for them to write or draw their impressions. Kids find these great fun to complete. In the hunt for dads, for example, the 1636 picture of *The Saltonstall Family* is in stark contrast to 1978's *Melanie & Me Swimming*, though in some ways they are very similar.

KEEP IN MIND
For those still in an art frenzy, it doesn't come much wilder than Tate Modern, in its powerful, huge new home. You can take the Art Bus there (a "riverbus" is also planned); check at the Information Desk for availability.

HEY, KIDS! The two biggest geniuses of British landscape painting (pictures representing natural scenery) are generally considered to be Constable and Turner. You can find the world's best collection of their works here, in the Clore Gallery. They both painted in the early 19th century, but what is even more surprising is that they both chose to focus their paintings on the same picturesque part of England—the counties of Norfolk and Suffolk, known collectively as East Anglia.

TATE MODERN

As art galleries go, this is the best for kids. The building once housed a power station, and in its state-of-the-art conversion, the central space was kept to its original massive proportions—great for displaying large, towering, wacky pieces of sculpture. Just walking in gives you the sense that anything can happen, and, as you soon discover at this off-the-wall, modern-art museum, it does.

There are several choices in children's programs. Kids like the audio trail, which explores selected pieces in the landscape gallery, from Long's ring of red granite stones on the gallery floor and his photos of fields of daisies to Monet's classic lily pond. You might think these are miles apart, but both have similar aims. Poems, music, and artists' and kids' points of view—no arty-speak here—prompt children to look at art in fun ways, determine their own opinions, and really get involved. They also learn about techniques created by groundbreaking artists, such as in Matisse's snail collage and Jackson Pollock's squiggles. Not only do kids find these pieces wild and attractive, they are

KEEP IN MIND Starters is a free innovative workshop run by artists for kids 5 and up accompanied by an adult. The workshops are offered every Saturday afternoon at 2, as well as on other days during vacations. Check with the information desk for details.

EATS FOR KIDS The spacious **Café** (Level 2, tel. 020/7401–5413), actually on the ground floor, has floor-to-ceiling windows overlooking the river and St. Paul's Cathedral. The British-accented menu includes seasonal dishes—light grills with salads in summer, casseroles and root-vegetable mash in winter—followed by British cheeses or to-die-for desserts. Children find plenty of pasta and meat dishes. Alternatively, pick up picnic supplies from the **Espresso Bar** (Level 4) or **McKraze Sandwich Emporium** (59 Upper Ground, tel. 020/7928–6450), at Hatfields and Upper Ground. Also see *Golden Hinde*, Millennium Bridge, and Shakespeare's Globe.

 Bankside, SE1. Tube: Blackfriars, London
Bridge, Southwark

 Free

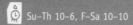 Su–Th 10–6, F–Sa 10–10

 020/7887–8008; www.tate.org.uk

 7 and up

encouraged to think about what the artist might (or might not) have been trying to achieve. Parents can join in the fun, too.

Start is a program specifically for families looking around the gallery together. Pick up a map and bag of games and puzzles on Level 3, and set off on your journey. You can take as little or as long as you want, but when you've finished, you can stick your impressions and drawings on the wall—actually having your work hung in one of the world's largest modern-art galleries. If you'd rather take your work and ideas away with you, try the Explorers family trails, available from the information desk. These focus on small sections of the gallery; you might make your own time capsule, for instance, or be an art critic, with help from a folder that suggests different viewpoints. Whatever you do, you'll find your trip here explores art at its interactive and thoughtful best.

HEY, KIDS! While the building was being renovated, workmen would arrive in the morning to be greeted by a family of foxes, who had made their home in the disused power station—quite a strange sight in this busy urban area. The foxes were given an alternative home, but pigeons refused to leave. It's become even more of a problem now that millions of visitors leave crumbs outside. On most Fridays, long before visitors arrive, a black hawk (kept especially for the job) is let out on the roof to scare the pesky birds and keep them from making a permanent roost.

THAMES BARRIER VISITOR CENTRE

For maximum impact, arrive by boat to appreciate the great hulk that is the Thames Barrier, an amazing structure that resembles a set of humongous shiny steel shells positioned in a defensive line across the river. It's defensive not in the military sense, but because London has recorded "gret wyndes and fluddes" as far back as 1099. In 1236 you could actually row a boat inside Westminster Hall. As water levels have risen each century, coupled with a surge tide when the North Sea rises and increases the tidal flow of the Thames estuary, a flood barrier became necessary.

In the visitor center, start with a film that describes the history in lively detail, with fabulous fire and water effects that appear to engulf the stage. With history pumping in your brain, find out all there is to know about the river's life and how the barrier was conceived and engineered through yet another film, in a small, yet intensively interactive exhibit area. Play with a set of telephones that serve as a mock barrier control center, and turn handles and push buttons to discover more about the river and its diverse life—

EATS FOR KIDS The **Riverside Terrace Café** (tel. 020/8854–8028) has sandwiches, ices, and snacks, but if you want a bigger refuel and greater options, go to Greenwich, home to riverside pubs and village restaurants (*see Cutty Sark*). Thames Path walkers are amply rewarded at the cozy, nautical **Cutty Sark** (Ballast Quay, tel. 020/8858–3146), a pub at journey's end. A hostelry has stood here since 1695, but this building is only 200 years old; the eponymous ship is a good ½ mile farther. Tables practically on the river have wonderful views across to Canary Wharf and the Docklands (*see above*), and food features stuffed Yorkshire puddings.

 1 Unity Way, Woolwich, SE18.
Rail: Charlton

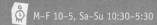 £3.40 ages 17 and up,
£2 children 5–16

020/8305–4188;
www.environment-agency.gov.uk

 M–F 10–5, Sa–Su 10:30–5:30

4 and up

from salmon to mollusks—an improvement since 1962, when the river was so polluted that nothing survived. An artificial smell gives a hint of how nasty it could get back in 1856, before there were sewage systems. A computer section follows the history of Old Father Thames and other aspects of life on the riverbank.

By now you'll want to get onto one of the barrier pier sections, but, due to security, that's not possible. The best way to get close is to take one of the frequent boats from Greenwich or Westminster, which pass between the piers. Still, the view from the riverside shows the powerful industrial architecture, and a good playground and picnic area on the grassy riverbank looks out on boats passing through the barrier and airplanes landing at London City Airport, on the opposite shore.

HEY, KIDS! Want to know what it was like for the diving engineers who worked on the riverbed building the barrier's foundations? Jump inside the large white square cell in the mini playground. Then imagine it shut and surrounded by the pressure of the water. Feeling comfortable?

KEEP IN MIND Campion Launches (tel. 020/8305–0300) operates 30-minute boat trips to the barrier from Greenwich Pier, late February–late October. Service from Westminster via Canary Wharf is run by Thames Cruises (tel. 020/7930–3373). Both operators give accompanying tour commentary. The barrier marks the eastern end of the Thames Path (see Docklands), an alternative route back to Greenwich; allow about an hour. The London Walking Forum has a good Web site (www.londonwalking.com), where you can discover a huge web of walks that crisscross and encircle London and its outer green spaces.

THEATRE MUSEUM

Who let the *Cats* out? London's national museum of theater contains all sorts of exhibits and activities that teach about the theater and its associated techniques.

Take, for example, the face painting. Stage makeup artists will create any fantasy face you want (for free); so, for example, a little girl can be transformed into a fairy-tale mermaid. Meanwhile, you can watch a video that shows how the gruesome makeup for *Phantom of the Opera* is put together, layer upon layer. Now imagine singing for a couple of hours with all that hardened goo around your mouth. Your youngster might also be able to take part in a dress-up session, using a fabulous range of theatrical costumes from the small studio theater downstairs. On the less showy side, you can find out about early Chinese shadow puppetry and how to make your own little theater and puppets. Check out the available activities at the entrance.

HEY, KIDS!
Remember the tale of Tom Thumb? He was a real person: an American-born midget who used to entertain Queen Victoria. The museum has the elaborate teeny waistcoat he used to wear and a picture of him, performing on a table at a party.

EATS FOR KIDS **Tuttons** (11–12 Russell St., tel. 020/7836–4141), facing the piazza, has a brasserie menu that includes steak, Thai chicken, club sandwiches, fries, and fab desserts. For most dishes, smaller portions for kids are available on request. In summer, sit outside and watch the street musicians, mime artists, and passersby. **Maxwell's** (8–9 James St., tel. 020/7836–0303), opposite the museum, serves up burgers plus. For a truly British, no-frills filling meal, walk north on Bow Street to **Rock and Sole Plaice** (47 Endell St., tel. 020/7836–3785); fish-and-chips have been sold on this site for over 100 years. Also see *Covent Garden*.

 7 Russell St, WC2.
Tube: Covent Garden

 020/7836-7891;
www.theatremuseum.org

 £4.50 ages 17 and up,
£2.50 students

 T–Su 11–7

 7 and up

The ground floor is devoted to a special long-running exhibition, usually interactive, which looks at different aspects of theater. The rest of the museum—corridors that resemble a rabbit warren in the bowels of an auditorium—traces the history of theater, including Shakespeare, such great actors as Henry Irving and Sarah Bernhardt, costumes, and programs. Free tours are absorbing for adults, but the high point for children might very well be the video and exhibit on how the Royal National Theatre (*see above*) staged the classic *Wind in the Willows*. With Alan Bennett's (the scriptwriter's) soothing tones in the background, you find out how a bunch of actors become a gang of sleazy, double-dealing stoats and weasels. It's all in the body movement: the flick of the head, the curl of the lip, the slide-skip walk, and a bit of a cor-blimey (cockney) accent. It's completely convincing, even in rehearsal, without a hint of face paints.

KEEP IN MIND   Children's workshops and demonstrations, directly linked to the major exhibition on the ground floor, are often given. These usually cover areas on the slightly wilder side of theater, such as the carnival and animation. Check on the board outside the building entrance for details. Stage Truck, a program of themed activity workshops—with things to make and do and ways to look at the museum more closely—runs during summer vacation (late July–early September).

THORPE PARK

For the wildest way to get wet west of London, hop on this series of rides that include all possible forms of splashing and that suit all ages and inclinations, from hardened thrill-riders to tinies and nervous parents. Even if you spend all day here, you won't cover everything.

The highlight is the Tidal Wave, a huge water slide dominating the center of the park, but imaginatively set in a small fishing village in New England about to experience a freak disaster. It looks more frightening than it is. To assault your senses (but stay dry), Pirates 4-D is a swashbuckling film show with fantastic 3-D special effects. If you can't stand the sensation of bats or insects flapping in your face, loud sounds, and a vibrating floor, avoid it. It's all very surreal and, despite the hammy acting, immense fun. The other mindblower is the ride entitled X:\No Way Out. Baffled by the name? That's nothing compared to what happens inside. After wandering through dimly lit tunnels, including a revolving neon drum with disorientating lighting and sound effects, you are thrown into a journey through the

KEEP IN MIND Wise kids wear their swimming gear underneath light clothes that dry quickly after a soaking. Of course, if the weather's nice and warm, who cares about getting (and staying) wet? For those who don't like getting drenched, waterproof ponchos are on sale for £2.50. Since tickets are quite expensive and the park is quite large, you should arrive early to make the most of your day and avoid the lines for the popular rides, which get even longer as the day progresses.

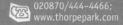 Staines Rd., Chertsey, Surrey

020870/444-4466;
www.thorpepark.com

£18.50 ages 15 and up, £14.50
children 5 (or over 1 meter)–14;
£2 discount for advance reservations

 Early Apr–late Oct,
M–F 10 (9:30 school vacations)–5,
Sa–Su 9:30–7:30

3 and up

night sky. The very weird and sensational ride makes you feel you're lost in space,
so it's not recommended for the nervous (or after a big lunch).

By comparison, Thunder River offers plain water fun without fear; it's like a
condensed white-water rafting expedition. To dry out and slow down the pace,
take the train ride over to Thorpe Farm, where you can pet the animals and take
a boat ride back. Or chill out by the "beach" and take the super-elevated Depth
Charge undulating water slide.

By opening new rides, the theme park strives to keep up with the latest in
technological thrills. Adults and observant older kids may find that some of
the older-style rides seem a little tame, but, in the main, there is plenty to
keep veteran theme-parkers happy. And if the usual volume of kids' screams
is anything to go by, there's obviously enough shriekable stuff for everyone.

EATS FOR KIDS

Unless you bring your own picnic (and there are many places
to enjoy it), you'll have to choose
from fast-food everything, from
Burger King and **KFC** to
Donuts.

GETTING THERE Thorpe Park is off the M25 freeway, which loops
around London. Take exit 11 or 13 (not 12, as this puts you onto another freeway),
and follow the signs. The entrance is off the A320 trunk road. By rail, catch a train
from Waterloo station to Staines. From there it's a short taxi ride (10 minutes) or a
half-hour walk.

TOWER BRIDGE EXPERIENCE

The Tower Bridge is one of those landmarks that's a magnet for every tourist, but few actually venture inside it. Here's your chance to walk in its hallowed tower and discover the secrets behind its history and enduring appeal. Enter from the north side, by the Tower of London, and allow about 1½–2 hours for a good visit—especially fun for kids who like nautical stuff, history, and how things work.

To unravel the bridge's story from the beginning—including some history of the river—follow a special route with videos and animatronics led by Harry the chirpy chappie painter. Kids who like to flit from screen to display in whatever order the mood takes them won't get as much out of this, but it does provide a sense of time and place. The bridge was constructed in 1894, when the Port of London was thriving and large trading ships came up the river to unload their goods. Its design had to allow for river traffic, the increasing number of vehicles that were passing between the north and south banks, and pedestrians. The answer was a liftable "bascule" (drawbridge) design that had a pedestrian walkway

HEY, KIDS!
Imagine an airplane flying underneath the high-level walkway! It happened once. Luckily, no one was hurt, but not surprisingly the pilot lost his job—even though he had the temerity to pull off the stunt.

KEEP IN MIND The royal yacht *Brittania* passed through the lifted bridge on its last voyage, and though you'll never see that sight again, you can still see the bridge lifted regularly. To find out if an opening might coincide with your itinerary, call 020/7378–7700 for information on the upcoming week. During the summer and other school vacations, free crafts workshops for kids are offered. One such is kite making—what better place to fly a kite than by the river! Combination tickets with the Monument (*see above*) are available.

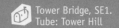
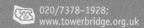
Tower Bridge, SE1.
Tube: Tower Hill

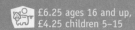
£6.25 ages 16 and up,
£4.25 children 5–15

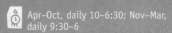
Apr–Oct, daily 10–6:30; Nov–Mar,
daily 9:30–6

020/7378–1928;
www.towerbridge.org.uk

6 and up

beneath the spires of the two towers, which house the massive machinery. In the engine room, you can see the old preserved hydraulics (electric controls are now used) with hands-on exhibits that demonstrate how the whole thing swings into life, with gears, spans, and lots of huge shiny cylinders.

Older kids might find the touch-screen section a little tame, but they should find at least some thrills in the history and in walking across the pedestrian walkway. Smaller kids have to be lifted to get a good view, but what a view it is! Photographs show how the area has changed over the years and what you can spot today. No doubt a return visit will reveal even more, since Thames-side development keeps powering ahead, and this part of the river continues to regenerate.

EATS FOR KIDS   South of the river, set among very upscale restaurants in design-conscious Butlers Wharf, **Ask** (Butlers Wharf, tel. 020/7403–4545) serves pasta in smaller child's portions (from £3.50) and pizzas in the usual size (from £4.30). It boasts great river views and the modern, stream-lined, chrome surroundings so prevalent in Italianate eateries. In summer you can sit outside. Also see Tower of London.

TOWER OF LONDON

S end him to the Tower!" That royal command filled many a prisoner with dread, and those who entered by Traitors' Gate, on the Thames, were unlikely to return. The Tower actually comprises many different towers, added through the centuries. It has been a fortress, medieval palace, royal prison, and even the royal menagerie, the basis for the London Zoo. The original White Tower was built by the French duke William the Conqueror, who had it constructed to impress the natives; 900 years later it impresses tourists.

The Crown Jewels are a more modern addition (from 1660), but their splendor is no less staggering, as lines testify. Head to the Jewel House first; once through the thick strong-room doors, you watch film of historic coronations. Then it's on to the real things: crowns bursting with jewels, scepters, rings, and other priceless paraphernalia whose diamonds are the size of minimuffins. The Queen's Imperial State Crown and scepter (with the world's largest cut diamond) are still used each November for the State Opening of Parliament. To find out how they were made, visit the Martin Tower's Crowns and Diamonds exhibit.

KEEP IN MIND To avoid lining up for tickets, buy them from any Underground station. Another way to miss the worst crowds is to arrive early. (Allow at least three hours to explore.) At the entrance, pick up a children's work sheet (available during school vacations) and check the schedule of daily events and guided Yeoman Warder tours. These centuries-old guards (also called Beefeaters) wearing the familiar red-and-gold uniforms generally lead tours daily (subject to weather) and at no charge; tours leave from the Middle Tower about every 30 minutes until 3:30 in summer, 2:30 in winter.

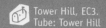
Tower Hill, EC3.
Tube: Tower Hill

020/7709-0765 voice,
020/7680-9004 recording;
www.hrp.org.uk

£11 ages 16 and up,
£8.30 students,
£7.30 children 5-15

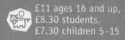
Mar-Oct, M-Sa 9-6, Su 10-6;
Nov-Feb, T-Sa 9-5, Su-M 10-5;
last entry 1 hr before closing

5 and up

Aristocratic traitors were imprisoned in the Beauchamp Tower, where they killed time chiseling artistic graffiti in the walls. Only lords and ladies were beheaded here, and they're listed behind the executioner's block on Tower Green. The headless ghost of Anne Boleyn, Henry VIII's second wife, is said to walk by with her entourage. To get an idea of what life was like, go to the Wakefield Tower, where costumed guides answer questions and tell tales of those sometimes terrible times. Weapons fanatics find the elaborate displays of flintlock pistols and swords in the White Tower absorbing. Check out the armor, particularly Henry VIII's extra-extra-large size and miniversions for little princes, and the old arsenal, where gunpowder barrels line the walls. Thankfully, the Great Fire stopped short; if it hadn't, they would have had a truly explosive fireworks show and we would have been deprived of this fascinating glimpse into the past.

EATS FOR KIDS
The **New Armouries Restaurant** serves fresh food courtesy of chef Digby Trout and old-world recipes. The interior looks much like the original horse armory. Outside the tower, two **Pret a Manger** stands sell good sandwiches and snacks, but you may have to fight off some hungry pigeons.

HEY, KIDS! The Tower has ghost stories galore. The tale of the young Princes Edward and Richard, who died in 1483, is the saddest one. The story goes that they stand holding hands in their nightgowns before fading into the walls of the Bloody Tower. Another has it that not even dogs will go into the Salt Tower after dark, and a third asserts that a Yeoman Warder was once almost throttled by an unseen force. After visiting the Tower, you can decide whether to believe them or not.

VICTORIA & ALBERT MUSEUM

5

Outside the V&A, old-guard English greats including Turner, Constable, and Wren are sculpted high in the exterior wall. Inside, a swirling, snakelike chandelier by Dale Chihuly (1999) hangs in vibrant blue-and-green glass. It's a stark contrast demonstrating that old and new are both at home in the world's ultimate collection of decorative arts.

Decorative arts are anything and everything that adorns buildings and bodies, from furniture to textiles, from Christian Dior outfits from the 1940s and Mary Quant's 1960s miniskirts in the Dress section to samurai armor and ancient Japanese weaponry as intricately decorated as it was deadly. In the India gallery, Tipoo's Tiger, a carved wooden instrument painted in bright colors, seems funny enough, until you notice that the tiger is mauling an Englishman to death; perhaps the owner wanted to have a go at the Brits. Even more ancient is the reproduction of Trajan's Column (AD 113) in the Plaster Casts gallery. The frieze that wraps around the towering column measures an astounding 200 meters (650 feet) and features more than 2,500 sculpted figures

KEEP IN MIND Allow at least two hours here. To visit cheaply, come after 4:30, when admission is free. (To stretch your visit, come on Wednesday, when the museum is open late.) The downside is that generally just the ground floor is open and kids' backpacks aren't available.

EATS FOR KIDS The excellent **V&A Restaurant,** in the pretty bricked basement, has a budget-price "hungry monkey" kids' menu, including such favorite staples as chicken, sausages, potatoes, and baked beans, followed by a daily dessert. On Sundays you can enjoy brunch or lunch while listening to music performed by students from the nearby Royal College of Music. **Patisserie Valerie** (215 Brompton Rd., tel. 020/7823–9971), toward Harrods, serves pasta dishes of the day. It's famed for its mountainous chocolate cakes, but service can be a little curt.

Cromwell Rd., South Kensington, SW7.
Tube: South Kensington

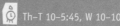
Th–T 10–5:45, W 10–10

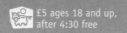
£5 ages 18 and up,
after 4:30 free

020/7942–2000;
www.vam.ac.uk

4 and up

in celebration of the emperor's war campaigns. Getting a close look at each battling gladiator is amazing.

V&A could just as easily stand for variety and activity, as the museum has award-winning programs for families. At the information desk, you can pick up free children's trail sheets (to work on with adults) any day but Sunday and during school vacations. An activity cart bears assignment trays with fun things to do, such as making masks or pictures with paper, sequins, and shiny stick-ons. Each week the cart highlights a different section of the museum. To explore some of the 7 miles of galleries in depth, ask for an activity backpack, filled with goody bags and folders to follow with an adult. In the Glass gallery, for instance, you can see in different dimensions with a pair of magic glasses, feel objects while blindfolded and then hunt for the original, and put together a jigsaw. It's great fun; the only problem is that you won't have enough time or energy to complete the six backpacks available.

HEY, KIDS! In the China gallery, look for a pair of cute silk embroidered slippers. You might think that they must have belonged to a doll, but the truth is that footwear like this was actually once worn by adult women. Their feet were bound at an early age so they would remain tiny enough to fit into shoes like this. (Needless to say, it wasn't very good for the feet.) Thankfully, binding feet is not done today.

WALLACE COLLECTION

Lady Wallace left this wonderful collection of art to the people on the condition that admission would remain free, but that's just one of many reasons to visit. Another is the collection's elegant setting: Hertford House, an oasis of calm and elegance just behind bustling Oxford Street. Walking around in the house and surveying the collection, which belonged to one family, the Marquesses of Hertford, you feel as if you've received a prized invitation to tour the family heirlooms. The collection includes a brilliant concentration of famed artists: Canaletto, Rubens, Rembrandt, and Velázquez, to name a few. Prime among the must-see list is Frans Hals's *The Laughing Cavalier,* a jolly fellow if ever there was one.

A recent renovation has been accompanied by the addition of trail booklets. For a small price (80p–£1), these invite parents and kids to walk around and talk about the paintings, furniture, and treasures and discover some fun facts. Adult notes let you help kids out and learn more yourself. Choose from the Monster trail; Paws and Claws, for younger kids; or

KEEP IN MIND Activity sessions during school vacations last 1½–2 hours and cost £5. Each is geared to a specified age range, and unless your kids are at the top of that range, they must be accompanied by an adult (who is not charged). To book in advance, call tel. 020/7563–9551. Older kids might like the free 20-minute Brief Encounter sessions, generally at 1, which celebrate one particular work. Free one-hour guided tours of the gallery depart Wednesday and Saturday at 11:30, Sunday at 3, and other days at 1. Times may change if there is a special lecture.

Hertford House, Manchester Sq., W1.
Tube: Bond St.

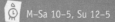 Free

 M–Sa 10–5, Su 12–5

020/7563–9516;
www.wallace-collection.org.uk

6 and up

Liberty, Equality and Fraternity, a family trail on the French Revolution, for older kids. On the subject of battle and strife, one of the best parts of the Wallace is secreted in the basement. Here you can see one of the country's finest collections of armor, containing the suits of many princes. If you want to see how different pieces might fit, head to the Conservation Room for a try.

To really visit the Wallace in a hands-on way, come when there's a children's activity session (about two hours; book in advance). Artists, sculptors, storytellers, and puppet makers help kids take a closer look at paintings with a particular theme, such as heroes and heroines or long-ago parties. Having been fired up with ideas from around the gallery, children produce their own piece of art. They may even get to try on some of that fabulous armor—all making for a memorable visit.

HEY, KIDS! Only people with loads of money could afford to have their portrait done by one of the top painters of the day, such as Velazquez or Rembrandt. And since you paid by the yard, only the extremely wealthy opted for life-size dimensions.

EATS FOR KIDS **Café Bagatelle** (tel. 020/7563–9505), in the bright new courtyard, is run by top London chef Stephen Bull. Although it's a lovely place to eat, it's pricey and not geared toward kids. Lunch would come in at around £20 per person. Luckily, there are many budget alternatives nearby: **Stockpot** (50 James St., tel. 020/7486–9185), for spaghetti, bakes, and daily specials; **Wagamama** (101A Wigmore St., tel. 020/7409–0111), a modern noodle bar; and **Browns** (47 Maddox St., tel. 020/7491–4565), well worth the walk for the all-day breakfast and memorable puds (puddings), Brit-style.

WESTMINSTER ABBEY

3

A beautiful Early English Gothic showpiece with flying buttresses and sweeping arches, Westminster Abbey has hosted coronations since 1066 and is stuffed with royal tombs, monuments, and memorials to prominent people. From floor to fabulously decorated ceiling, there's plenty to admire.

The ancient Chapel of St. Edward (where the founder king is buried) is encircled by worn effigies of medieval monarchs, missing mosaic stones stolen for souvenirs over the centuries. Sadly, it's so worn that you're not permitted inside. Beneath the steps to the Henry VII Chapel, the Coronation Chair bears the graffiti of naughty Westminster schoolboys. Inside the Henry VII Chapel, which is dominated by the tombs of King Henry and his queen (Elizabeth), Elizabeth I, her sister Mary I (beneath her), and Mary Queen of Scots (opposite aisle) are entombed as well. A marble urn contains the bones of the young princes presumed murdered in the Tower of London (*see above*), and choir stalls contain curious carved creatures. Poets' Corner is crammed full of memorials and visitors. Noteworthy denizens

HEY, KIDS!
Take a closer look at the little round splotches in the granite pillars. They're actually fossilized mollusks—just one of the neat details to discover here.

KEEP IN MIND Photography is not allowed within the abbey, but pictures can be found in the stunning color guidebooks and postcards on sale at the Abbey Bookshop, outside the west entrance, and in the Abbey Museum. These show many of the sacred and ancient places not often open to visitors, such as St. Edward's Chapel. If you particularly want to take a closer look at these areas, sign up for a Verger tour (£3), well worth the extra charge. Phone for information, or check on the information board outside the entrance.

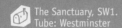 The Sanctuary, SW1.
Tube: Westminster

 Abbey £6 ages 16 and up,
£2 children 11–15; Chapter
House, Pyx Chamber, and
museum extra

 Abbey M–F 9–3:45, Sa 9–12:45, closed for
some services; Chapter House and museum
daily 9:30–5; Pyx Chamber daily 9:30–4

020/7222–5152;
www.westminster-abbey.org

 6 and up

are Handel, Dickens, Byron, Wilde, and Shakespeare. Scientists Newton, Darwin, and Livingstone are in the nave, near Ben Jonson (buried standing up, per his wishes, but without a coffin as he couldn't afford one). The Tomb of the Unknown Warrior is near eight volumes listing citizens who died during the Blitz.

The Abbey Museum almost brings tomb residents to life through startlingly realistic effigies: Henry VII's was taken from his death mask; Charles II's, equally realistic, is richly adorned; and Elizabeth I's is displayed in underwear. Search for the ring she gave to her favorite, Essex, along with its romantic story. The Pyx Chamber, next door, is in its near-original state. Here you can hold a weighty key that secured gold and silver, as part of a kids' activity sheet. The renovated Chapter House (where a religious chapter was read daily) still has its ancient tiled floor with medieval images. Joining these rooms to the abbey, the cloister is a quiet haven where you can reflect on the rich history of this ancient place.

EATS FOR KIDS Victoria Street runs the full gamut of chain eateries, from pizzas places and burger joints to **Starbucks** (137 Victoria St., tel. 020/7233–5170) and **Pret a Manger** (75B Victoria St., tel. 020/7222–1020), for snacks and coffee. By way of a change, the pine-and-glass **Army and Navy department store restaurant** (101 Victoria St., tel. 020/7834–1234) is light and airy. Children's meals consist of the usual: fries with sausages, chicken nuggets, or fish sticks for £1.99. For parents, a daily changing menu includes vegetarian dishes from £4.95. Also see Royal Mews at Buckingham Palace.

WIMBLEDON LAWN TENNIS MUSEUM

For two weeks in June each year, Britons and other fans are gripped with tennis fever, as the titans slug it out on grass in one of the world's most coveted tennis championships. When it all began, in the early 1900s, there were no professionals and no big prize money. Back then, it was a genteel, fashionable game for the upper classes, a craze on the lawns of polite society in Victorian England. The club held its own informal amateur championships among about 10 participants. Today, those who love the game can make a pilgrimage to this museum and tennis mecca.

You can browse through all sorts of memorabilia, including old-time outfits, which look like they were meant more for a posh picnic than thrashing around on the court. Do you think Venus Williams would look dynamic in ankle-length linen instead of skimpy Lycra? How fast could Pete Sampras serve with a funny-looking wooden racket with gappy strings rather than titanium technology? You can gaze upon the authentic championship trophies and marvel that, in the old amateur days, after all that sweaty effort, the winners only

EATS FOR KIDS The **Café Centre Court** is open year-round and serves snacks, lunch, and traditional tea in a nostalgic setting of wood paneling, murals, and conservatory-style furniture. Options on the High Street in Wimbledon village are many. They include **Starbucks** (82 High St., tel. 020/8947–5577), **Pizza Express** (84 High St., tel. 020/8946–6027), **Café Pasta** (8 High St., tel. 020/8944–6893), and **Nachos** (36 High St., tel. 020/8944–8875), whose names all speak for themselves.

All England Lawn Tennis & Croquet Club,
Church Rd., Wimbledon, SW19.
Tube: Southfields

 Museum £5 ages 17 and up,
£4 children 5–16; tour
£10 ages 17 and up, £9 children.

 Daily 10:30–5

 020/8946–6131;
www.wimbledon.org

 5 and up

got a medal. A model shows how Wimbledon looked back then, videos let you relive great games of the past, and an interactive quiz tests your knowledge of the tournament and its competitors. You can even try to buy tickets for next year's tournament, but good luck! You must apply in writing months in advance, and tickets for the singles finals are extremely hard to come by.

You can ask questions of guides in old-style tennis gear who are on hand to highlight the displays, scheduled to be updated for the 2001 championships. An even better idea is to reserve a spot in one of the small-group tours. In addition to seeing the museum, you get a real peek behind the scenes, get close to the show courts' sacred turf, and take a look around the broadcast studios. It may be the closest you'll get to Centre Court unless your tennis game improves dramatically.

HEY, KIDS! Strawberries and cream are synonymous with Wimbledon. Come rain or shine, the Championships pretty much herald the start of the English strawberry-eating season. Each year at the tournament, a mountainous 23 tons of strawberries are consumed—at a price, of course!

WINDSOR CASTLE

In 1080, William the Conqueror chose a good place for his fortress, close to the Thames and London. Though the stone castle has grown much over the centuries, it remains the only castle that has been constantly used by the royal family since William's day. Today it still dominates the landscape, towering above the pretty town of old Windsor and neighboring Eton, across the Thames, and it can clearly be seen from the freeway heading west from London. Whether viewed from inside or out, Windsor Castle is spectacular.

Children do find parts of the castle interior fascinating. The fabulously ornate State Apartments contain old master paintings, chintz, china, and chandeliers galore, but the Grand Staircase and Vestibule's old weaponry—shiny swords, muskets and rifles in cases, and crisscrossed weapons hung on very high walls—will probably entice kids far more. You can see Henry VIII's armor of massive girth and the very bullet that killed Lord Nelson at the Battle of Trafalgar. One of the oldest rooms, St. George's Hall, was beautifully

HEY, KIDS!

Like all the royals, Britain's queens have retreated to Windsor Castle. Queen Victoria and her nine children got away from smoky London on the new steam railway and received diplomats and dignitaries here. You'll know the current Queen is in if the Royal Standard is flying.

KEEP IN MIND It's worth phoning to check on opening times and whether the State Apartments are closed for a royal banquet. Arrive early to avoid lines and give yourself time to absorb the charms of old Windsor and Eton. Even if you don't visit the castle, you can spend a lovely day at the Eton Brocas, the pretty meadows sloping down to the river, where you can watch boats, royal swans, and ducks go by, or in the extensive grounds of Windsor Great Park, where you might catch a polo match or spy a herd of shy deer in the old royal hunting grounds.

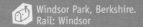 Windsor Park, Berkshire.
Rail: Windsor

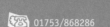 01753/868286

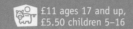 £11 ages 17 and up,
£5.50 children 5–16

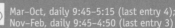 Mar–Oct, daily 9:45–5:15 (last entry 4);
Nov–Feb, daily 9:45–4:50 (last entry 3)

 All ages

restored after a fire in 1992. It's lined with knights in armor bearing lances pointing up to the ceiling, which is emblazoned with the coats of arms of all the Knights of the Garter. At one end, the royal champion knight is poised, gauntlet raised, ready to throw down a challenge; this wasn't a usual occurrence but rather a coronation ritual.

The most charming item is a dollhouse made for Queen Mary (Queen Elizabeth's grandmother), at the entrance to the State Apartments. Absolutely everything in the mansion was a faithful copy of 1924 furnishings, all of which work, from the electric lights and elevators to the gramophone. The cellar contains vintage wine, and books and paintings were produced by the authors and artists themselves. What little girl could resist playing with these minitreasures? It is positively enchanting, as are the larger doll's trousseaux belonging to the young Princesses Elizabeth and Margaret; designed by Dior and other great couturiers of the 1930s, they are displayed in the adjoining room.

EATS FOR KIDS There is nothing to eat within the castle, but old Windsor has plenty of choices. In the Fenwick department store, the **Terrace Café** (King Edward Ct., tel. 01753/855537), off Peascod Street and opposite Castle Hill, has a menu that changes daily. For some dishes, you can get half-portions for kids, including the usual favorite of sausage and fries. The old-world **Drury House** (4 Church St., tel. 01753/863734) has wood paneling, fireplaces, English roasts, traditional teas, and a warm welcome.

extra! extra!

THE CLASSICS

"I'M THINKING OF AN ANIMAL..." With older kids you can play 20 Questions: Have your leader think of an animal, vegetable, or mineral (or, alternatively, a person, place, or thing) and let everybody else try to guess what it is. The correct guesser takes over as leader. If no one figures out the secret within 20 questions, the first person goes again. With younger children, limit the guessing to animals and don't put a ceiling on how many questions can be asked. With rivalrous siblings, just take turns being leader. Make the game's theme things you expect to see at your day's destination.

"I SEE SOMETHING YOU DON'T SEE AND IT IS BLUE." Stuck for a way to get your youngsters to settle down in a museum? Sit them down on a bench in the middle of a room and play this vintage favorite. The leader gives just one clue—the color—and everybody guesses away.

FUN WITH THE ALPHABET

"*I'M GOING TO THE GROCERY...*" The first player begins, "I'm going to the grocery and I'm going to buy... " and finishes the sentence with the name of an object, found in grocery stores, that begins with the letter "A". The second player repeats what the first player has said, and adds the name of another item that starts with "B". The third player repeats everything that has been said so far and adds something that begins with "C" and so on through the alphabet. Anyone who skips or misremembers an item is out (or decide up front that you'll give hints to all who need 'em). You can modify the theme depending on where you're going that day, as "I'm going to X and I'm going to see..."

"*I'M GOING TO ASIA ON AN ANT TO ACT UP.*" Working their way through the alphabet, players concoct silly sentences stating where they're going, how they're traveling, and what they'll do.

FAMILY ARK   Noah had his ark—here's your chance to build your own. It's easy: Just start naming animals and work your way through the alphabet, from antelope to zebra.

WHAT I SEE, FROM A TO Z   In this game, kids look for objects in alphabetical order—first something whose name begins with "A", next an item whose name begins with "B", and so on. If you're in the car, have children do their spotting through their own window. Whoever gets to Z first wins. Or have each child play to beat his own time. Try this one as you make your way through zoos and museums, too.

PLAY WHILE YOU WAIT

NOT THE GOOFY GAME   Have one child name a category. (Some ideas: first names, last names, animals, countries, friends, feelings, foods, hot or cold things, clothing.) Then take turns naming things that fall into that category. You're out if you name something that doesn't belong in the category—or if you can't think of another item to name. When only one person remains, start again. Choose categories depending on where you're going or where you've been—historic topics if you've seen a historic sight, animal topics before or after the zoo, upside-down things if you've been to the circus, and so on. Make the game harder by choosing category items in A-B-C order.

DRUTHERS   How do your kids really feel about things? Just ask. "Would you rather eat worms or hamburgers? Hamburgers or candy?" Choose serious and silly topics—and have fun!

BUILD A STORY   "Once upon a time there lived..." Finish the sentence and ask the rest of your family, one at a time, to add another sentence or two. Bring a tape recorder along to record the narrative—and you can enjoy your creation again and again.

GOOD TIMES GALORE

WIGGLE & GIGGLE Give your kids a chance to stick out their tongues at you. Start by making a face, then have the next person imitate you and add a gesture of his own—snapping fingers, winking, clapping, sneezing, or the like. The next person mimics the first two and adds a third gesture, and so on.

JUNIOR OPERA During a designated period of time, have your kids sing everything they want to say.

THE QUIET GAME Need a good giggle—or a moment of calm to figure out your route? The driver sets a time limit and everybody must be silent. The last person to make a sound wins.

THE A-LIST

BEST IN TOWN
Tower of London
Tate Modern
Millennium Bridge
British Airways London Eye
Natural History Museum

BEST OUTDOORS
Legoland

BEST CULTURAL ACTIVITY
Hampton Court

BEST MUSEUM
Science Museum

WACKIEST
Hawk Conservancy/London Dungeon

NEW & NOTEWORTHY
Somerset House

SOMETHING FOR EVERYONE

TIRE THEM OUT

WATER, WATER EVERYWHERE

WAY UP HIGH

MANY THANKS!

More than once, I thought my two children (9 and 11) would rebel, as I faced them with yet another jam-packed weekend of visiting brilliant places in pursuit of the quintessential review. They didn't—rebel, that is—and had a ball, and so did their parents, who got to see many familiar sights in interesting new ways. So thank you, kids, for your enthusiasm and endurance during my persnickety investigations. My son was convinced I would turn into a National Geographic reporter as I picked up the trail of a new find. In the end, the limit of 68 places doesn't quite do London justice.

We also enjoyed especially attentive treatment from many attractions' education and information people, whose expert advice was a boon—in particular, the staff of the BFI London IMAX Cinema education department, BBC Experience, Bekonscot Model Village, Westminster Abbey, and English Heritage at the abbey's Chapter House. You provided a real personal touch. The press and publicity departments who ensured information packs were in the right place at the right time are too many to mention, as are the friends, relatives, and their children who reported faithfully on their missions and came back for more. What a team! Hopefully, the fruits of your labors will make other visitors' experiences all the more enjoyable.

And last, but no means least, Andrea Lehman, my editor, who has pulled it all together—including this writer—so that you could get out there and really enjoy.

–Jacqueline Brown